# TOXIC RELATIONSHIPS

*Understanding all types of toxicity will help you to find freedom. Learn to set guidelines with parents and people. You will learn to live a much more mentally healthy lifestyle*

**HOPE UTARAM**

Copyright © 2020 by *Hope Utaram*
- **All rights reserved** -

The content contained within this book may not be reproduced, duplicated or transmitted without direct written permission from the author or the publisher.

Under no circumstances will any blame or legal responsibility be held against the publisher, or author, for any damages, reparation, or monetary loss due to the information contained within this book. Either directly or indirectly.

Legal Notice:

This book is copyright protected. This book is only for personal use. You cannot amend, distribute, sell, use, quote or paraphrase any part, or the content within this book, without the consent of the author or publisher.

Disclaimer Notice:

Please note the information contained within this document is for educational and entertainment purposes only. All effort has been executed to present accurate, up to date, and reliable, complete information. No warranties of any kind are declared or implied. Readers acknowledge that the author is not engaging in the rendering of legal, financial, medical or professional advice. The content within this book has been derived from various sources. Please consult a licensed professional before attempting any techniques outlined in this book.

By reading this document, the reader agrees that under no circumstances is the author responsible for any losses, direct or indirect, which are incurred as a result of the use of the information contained within this document, including, but not limited to, — errors, omissions, or inaccuracies.

# Table of Contents

Introduction ................................................................1

Chapter 1 Comfortable With Not Knowing .............................14

Chapter 2 Causes Of Toxic/Negative Behavior........................ 24

Chapter 3 Setting Boundaries ................................................ 28

Chapter 4 Moving On............................................................ 37

Chapter 5 Acceptance ........................................................... 42

Chapter 6 The Roots Of Suffering ........................................... 49

Chapter 7 Free At Last .......................................................... 55

Chapter 8 The Toxic Termination Process (TTP).................... 74

Chapter 9 Exercises To Try ....................................................90

Chapter 10 Public And Private Images Of Narcissists ............ 101

Chapter 11 A Narcissistic Mother's Daughter ....................... 108

Chapter 12 Beating The Narcissists At Their Own Game ....... 114

Chapter 13 Statistics On Narcissistic Personality Disorder ....124

Conclusion ..........................................................................134

# Introduction

You will learn how to know about toxic relationships. How to know if your relationship is toxic. What to do about toxic parents and family.

Learning which of your friends and acquaintances are toxic and how to deal with them. If you have tried everything you know to do and still nothing happens, then it is okay to walk away.

Toxic relationships

Most of us have encountered a toxic person at one time in our life. These people are the ones that never fail to make you feel horrible about yourself. They do or say something that is serious about you. You might be in the best mood you've been in for a long time, and that one person says a sarcastic remark. It gives you a dirty look. They might have accused you of doing something to them or someone else that you would never do.

They have a knack of ruining your mood, your life, and your day. If you so much as challenge the way they think, they will blame you and everything immediately becomes your fault. You soon realize that once you have spent time with them, you will feel lousy. You are emotionally drained. You feel sick. You might sometimes experience being physically sick.

That's how people become known as toxic. A simple definition of toxic is poisonous. That makes these people poisonous to you. Now take it a step further. A simple definition of poison is any substance that results in injury to an organism or can destroy life. So, by these two definitions, toxic relationships could end your life because they can be extremely poisonous to you.

Toxic relationships are dangerous. They are depressing, irritating, obnoxious, and annoying. They could get your fired. They could ruin your reputation. They can bring down your spirits. They will chip away at your self-esteem. They will destroy any relationship you try to have. You will throw you into a deep depression. They will make you sick. You might start having panic or anxiety attacks, and your life will become miserable.

You are probably wondering how you can recognize these toxic individuals. Honestly, they are easy to spot. They will make you feel so bad just by being near them. You might have met someone and immediately knew they were toxic. You could sense their toxicity. Toxic relationships can be any size, shape, color, or age. Some toxic relationships might be hard to see at first, but with time, their true self is revealed.

We all have those toxic relationships that have dusted up with their poison. At times, we've been drenched. Difficult people are usually drawn to reasonable people. Some of us have had at least one person who has us bending like barbed wire trying to please them. Guess what, we never ever get there.

The damage they can do goes back to the way they sugar coat all responses to make you think you are the one who's wrong. They will make you question your tendency to misinterpret, oversensitivity, and over-reacting. If you are constantly hurt or changing your behavior when you are around them, then you are not at fault, they are.

Learning their harmful behavior is the first thing you need to do to make them stop hurting you. You can't change what they are doing, but you can change how you react to it. You can show them that they aren't getting away with hurting you anymore.

There are lots of things these toxic relationships try to do to manipulate situations and people to help them. Knowing the different types of person can help you from falling under their influence.

Here is a list of the various types of toxic relationships and descriptions of their characteristics.

The Psychopath: This person has absolutely no conscience, compassion, sympathy, or empathy. They don't feel remorse or guilt. They never learn from their mistakes and delight in seeing others suffer. They are very charismatic and charming. They can cast a spell over you before you know it. You will be drawn to them and their lies before you realize who and what they are. They will appear to be good, but in all reality, they are pure evil.

Every one of these people has two different personalities. One is nice. The other is evil. They can do massive amounts of damage everywhere they go, even possibly killing of others. These people are very abusive to their children and wives.

The Pathological Liar: This person will lie about everything. Lying is normal life for them. If they get caught in a lie, they will just tell a different one to cover up. They are capable of looking you right in your eyes and tell you a bold face lie without even blinking. They will walk away smug knowing you believed them.

They will lie to you before they apologize. There is no use in trying to argue with them. They will twist their stories. They will change what happened and retell it so that they start to believe their nonsense.

Don't think you are wrong just because you apologize. To move forward, you don't have to apologize. Just go on without them. You don't have to surrender to them. You don't have to keep arguing either. There just isn't any point. Most people would rather be right than be happy. There are better things to do than argue.

The Emotional Wreck: Everything is high drama with this person. They are constantly upset about something. Their thinking is way too extreme to think about life correctly. They blow everything way out of proportion. They are usually an emotional basket case. Their life is just one crisis after another. If they don't have a crisis at the moment, they will invent one.

They talk about it constantly and won't ever be interested in yours, just theirs.

These people will be nice one day, and the next day you will wonder what you did to upset them. There's usually not anything that caused the change in their attitude. You just automatically know that something is off. They could be cranky, cold, sad, or prickly if you ask them what's wrong. Their answer will usually be nothing. They will have a bit of an attitude with their answer to let you know that there is something wrong. This position could be shown by a raised eyebrow, a heavy sigh, or giving you the cold shoulder. If this happens, you could find yourself doing whatever you can to make them happy. You might even find yourself making excuses for their behavior. Now can you see why this works to their advantage?

You need to stop pleasing them. These people figured out that decent people will go to any length to keep these people happy. If you are doing everything in your power to make these people happy, then it is time to stop. Walk away. You can come back if the mood shifts. You aren't responsible for everyone's feelings. If you have done something unintentionally, then ask them about it. Talk to them about it. If you need to apologize, then by all means do. You should never have to guess what you have.

They will make up reasons as to why your news isn't good news. If you get a promotion, they will laugh at the amount of money you will be making. If you save money to go on vacation to the beach, they will make a snide comment about how hot it will be. It doesn't matter what you have accomplished in your life; they will find a way to make it sound less than it is. Do not let them bring you down to their level. You do not need to get their approval, or anyone's approval, ever.

The Joker: These will be the loudest people in the room. The make silly and crude jokes about others. They think they are funny. But in all reality, they are pathetic people. No one likes their sense of humor. They tell off-color jokes, at everyone's expense. They do this to take the attention off of them and their failures. This gives them the confidence they lack.

Mr. Negative: These are the most unpleasant people to have around you. They will find fault with everything and everyone. They have no joy. You might find yourself in a good mood, and they will do whatever necessary to bring you down. They always complain about everything and everyone. They have tremendous feelings of insecurity, jealousy, and hate.

Instead of owning their feelings, they will act like them are yours. This is called projection. They are projecting their feelings onto you. Someone that is angry but won't admit they are angry might blame you for being mad at them. It could be a subtle question asking why you are angry with them.

You will soon find yourself being on the defense and going around in circles. Know what emotions are yours and theirs. If you find you are defending yourself from their accusations, they are projecting their anger onto you. You do not have to defend, justify, or explain yourself. You do not have to deal with accusations. Just remember this.

The Moocher: This person is always asking to borrow anything and everything you have including cash. They will have memory loss when it comes time to pay back the loan. They will never make up for the favor.

Debbie Downer: This person is always in a bad mood. Debbie Downer will go to great lengths to stay in their bad mood. They will broadcast to anyone that will listen to them. This is all they will talk about. Every single negative thing that has ever happened to them. They will talk about what is happening to them and what could occur in the future. If you try to cheer them up or give them positive feedback, all they will have to say to you is "I agree, but..."

If you are trying to fix something that is important to you, Debbie Downers will bring up details from six months ago. They bring irrelevant information to the conversation that will confuse you and again make things look like it's your fault. You will find yourself defending yourself once again instead of dealing with what needs to be addressed. It always ends up being about what you have done.

The Slanderer: This is the most toxic. They will destroy lives and reputations with their lies. They constantly talk about everyone behind their backs, and this includes you.

We all mess up now and then, but the slanderer will let you know that you have. The judge you and dig at your self-esteem to make you think you are less just because you've made a mistake. You are allowed to be human and mess up now and then. If you haven't done anything to them personally, they have no reason to judge.

The Blackmailer: This person works hard to gain your trust and learn all your weaknesses and secrets then they will exploit you if you ever cross them. They are jealous of you but will pretend to be your friend. During all this time, they are making their plans of how to bring you down. They will appear to be trustworthy, but they are just the opposite. They will hold your mistakes over your head and threaten to tell your secrets to everyone if you don't do what they want. These people are very dangerous.

The Arguer: These people like causing fights. If there is a group discussing a certain topic and everyone agrees, this person will be the devil's advocate to get an argument started. They then sit back, smile, and enjoy the show. They will always ask a hateful question that will get a fight started. They are waiting for the moment to state an opposing view and reveal their agenda. When you get upset and try to defend yourself, they state that you are just too sensitive.

The Bully: This person gets an exhilaration out of threatening and intimidating others. They typically bully a person in front of a lot of individuals. They strut around knowing they are the center of attention. The look they get when they are bullying is very scary. You never know how far they are going to take the bullying or if the person being bullied is going to get hurt.

The Manipulator: These people always have a hidden agenda, and it's called control. They will think ahead and plan how they will manipulate someone to get their outcome. They will also confuse the situation at hand. Their malicious manipulations are evil and cunning.

You will hear you never or you always from these people. You cannot defend against this kind of manipulation. These people will draw on that one time you did something wrong. Do not get sucked into this argument. There is no way to win. And you don't need to.

They will always find a way to make you choose between them and what you need to do. You will always feel like you have to do for them. These people wait until you have a prior commitment and then they pounce. The problem is that no matter what you do for them enough is never enough. They are going to make it seem like it is always a matter of life and death, but chances are it won't be.

If you start to feel that you are the only contributing factor to your relationship, you are right. These people will send out a vibe telling you that you owe them something. They also find a way to take a thing from you that will hurt you. Then say to you to point blank that it is for your benefit. This is very common in relationships or workplaces where there is no balance of power. Like telling them, you left all the filing for them because they need the experience. Or inviting people for a dinner party and then expect your best friend to do all the cooking because they are a chef. You don't have to do anything for anybody. If it doesn't feel like it's happening for good, it isn't.

The Runaway: These people after having an argument with others, decide they are not going to pick up the phone to talk about it. They refuse to answer emails or texts. You will find yourself replaying the argument over in your head. You will start to second guess your relationship. You wonder what you did to upset them. You will even start to wonder if they are dead, alive, or ignoring you. This can all feel the same. People who truly care don't let you feel like rubbish without trying to sort it out. It doesn't mean it will get sorted out, but you will at least be trying. This is a sign of their commitment to the relationship when they leave you guessing for a long time.

The Mocker: These people might sound sincere, but their tone says much, much more. Asking someone what they did today can mean so many different things just by the way it was stated. It might say that you thought the person didn't do anything again today. It could convey that you thought their day was better than yours. If you ask them about the tone, they will get defensive and make the comment of it was just a simple question. When in all reality, it wasn't.

You may just be trying to get an issue resolved or clarify something, and in the blink of an eye, the conversation has taken a turn for the worse. It has moved from the matter to the way you are talking about it. It doesn't matter it was intentional or not. You will soon find you have to defend your words, gestures, tone and even the way your stomach moves as you breathe. I know that doesn't make sense. It doesn't need to make sense, but it does to them. Meanwhile, your need is gone to the big pile of unfinished conversation that grows bigger every single day.

Knowing how a toxic person usually will react to you make your radar sharper, and you will be able to spot them easier. If you know how to spot a toxic person, you might keep yourself from being sucked into their world. You won't have to tie yourself in knots to please them.

There are some people that no matter what you do, you can't please them. You will find that some people just aren't a good match for you and most of the times that has nothing to do with you. Don't be afraid to say no to crazy. Be confident in who you are, your quirks, your faults, and what makes you shine. You do not need anybody's approval. If someone is working overtime to manipulate you, then it is because they need you. You do no need them.

If these individuals are your families as your children, spouse, sister, brother, father, or mother, then it will be serious to you.

Do you remember what Jesus had to say about these people? He told his disciples to pick a town and preach the gospel. If the town chose to accept the disciples, everything was good. If the town decided to refuse the disciples and Jesus' teachings he told the disciples just to go on and don't worry about what the town had to say. Jesus told them to go where people would listen to them and take his teachings to heart. They did not need to jump through hoops to get people to listen.

This goes for the toxic relationships in your life. You are who you are. Your real friends will not treat you badly. You can just be yourself when you are around them. You don't need to pretend to be anyone else. You can do what you want and say what you want without fear of being manipulated, put down, or criticized. You can do this because they are not poisoned to you.

The main point is you absolutely cannot associate with the people who are trying to destroy you. They are destroying your happiness, peace, joy, and well-being without even using a weapon.

The best thing to do for these toxic relationships is to pray for them. Ask God to remove all the wickedness from the hearts and remove the crust from their eyes. Pray that they will be born again so their old ways can get replaced with a spirit of kindness and love. You cannot change them yourself. They are run by a darkness that belongs to the Devil. If they choose to follow Christ, the will see you as a friend. If they don't decide to follow Christ, they will see you an enemy. The Devil's goal is to destroy, steal, and kill. That is the same thing toxic relationships are doing to you. You and you alone can stop it.

# Chapter 1

## Comfortable With Not Knowing

Narcissists crave admiration and praise. You'll often see them fluttering about social gatherings with a smile plastered across their face, and with more than enough friendly chit-chat to go around. They're exceptionally talented at winning the hearts of acquaintances and friends with their charm and amiable demeanor, and they often take the spotlight at most parties and get-togethers.

With that, you might say that it's a bit of a challenge to find the narcissist, especially because many of us wouldn't think ill of someone who seems so well-adjusted in public spaces. In fact, there are times when those charming people we come across are really just friendly and charismatic, which doesn't necessarily indicate narcissism. So how can you figure out who the vampires are?

Keep these definitive markers in mind:

### They're Initially Likable

If you're meeting a person for the first time and you're worried they might turn out to be a narcissist, it's important to consider their likeability. At first glance, a narcissist can be incredibly friendly and fun to be with, offering great insight and wonderfully spontaneous conversation.

This is a common trait they all manifest because narcissists thrive on admiration and praise. They want to be noticed for their good qualities, so they'll put their best foot forward whenever meeting new people. Whether or not they get to maintain a relationship with you doesn't really matter – what they want is to make sure that everyone they come into contact with feels the same way about them – and that is that they're really friendly and likable.

Giving every new friend and acquaintance the same face creates a consistent image across all their contacts. Everyone they've ever talked to or dealt with has the same thing to say about them. So that must mean it's true, right?

If you've met someone who's just all rainbows and butterflies, does that confirm that they're a narcissist? Not really. There are some really well-rounded and well-adjusted people who are just naturally kind, friendly, and interesting, without any strings attached. What this simply means is that if you do meet someone who seems exceptionally likable, just keep your guard up and watch out for other possible signs.

## Conversations Always Circle Back to Them

Narcissists might seem like great conversationalists, especially if you're not necessarily guarded against them. But if you've got a heightened sense of narcissism in others, one thing you might notice is that all those great conversations somehow always manage to circle back to them.

You could start out talking about your cancer-ridden mother, and then suddenly find that you're talking about the narcissist's holiday getaway from last year. You could try to segue to your summer vacation plans, but you'll soon realize you're once again talking about their new kitchen remodeling project.

Oh yes, a narcissist can keep the conversation going because they like talking. But what you need to know is that they're mostly interested in talking about themselves. So as that conversation just keeps on going, you might realize that you've come to learn almost their entire history and all the great achievements and experiences they've had, with little room to interject with stories you want to share.

## They'll Overshare About Others

As you continue to talk to these narcissists, you'll notice that they know quite a lot about other people, and they won't be afraid to name drop. So even if you just met a few days ago and you're not too close to each other yet, you'll hear them dropping gossip about common people in your circle.

For someone who's not necessarily on the lookout for narcissists, all the juicy secrets could be reason enough to keep coming back and become even closer friends. After all, this is a likable, seemingly reliable person. So, they seem like a great source for this kind of information.

But, be wary. Often, narcissists get this information by talking directly with the people they gossip about, the same way they talk to you. Their friendly outward nature allows them to tap into the trust and comfort of others, so lots of people often feel safe sharing their secrets with these pretenders.

Whether or not your new friend is a narcissist, it's important that you guard your secrets since you can never tell who's willing to drop sensitive information that you share in confidence. With narcissists, the atmosphere of trust that they create can make it exceptionally easy to lay down even the most private details of your life. They can use this information later to degrade your image to common friends, and thus heighten their own 'polished' appearance.

## Issues with Envy

A common recurring theme that narcissists tend to talk about is envy. It's brought up in one of two ways: that there are people who are jealous of them, or that they're jealous of other people. When they express jealousy, however, it might not be as overt. This ties in with their tendency to talk about people behind their backs.

When a narcissist feels 'threatened' by someone else's assets – whether their career, good looks, financial status, or achievements – they'll likely try to water down that person's image and make them 'look bad.' In effect, they take out their competition, and win the crown as the most 'successful' or 'admirable' person in the lives of their friends and family.

For instance, Cristina who feels threatened by her sister Isabel's accomplishments might talk negatively about her behind her back. She might tell their cousins or common friends that Isabel is struggling through a problematic marriage, and that her children are defiant and destructively disobedient.

Most of the time, these 'half-truths' are simply inflated and made out to be much worse than they actually are. For example, the marital problems might be nothing more than the typical husband-wife banter that Cristina accidentally overhead during one of her visits. The 'defiant children' might have been a one-time occurrence when Isabel's eldest arrived home a little later than had been agreed.

Despite being partially untrue, she will continue to share this information with the common friends and family members they have in order to give the idea that Isabel's life isn't all that perfect. This deflects the praise she would have received, and thus makes Cristina look far more balanced and pleasant in comparison.

In a lot of ways, narcissists also tend to feel that others are particularly jealous of them. That's why they'll commonly use the statement "… because they're jealous of me," when trying to justify the actions of other people.

For instance, in the example above, Isabel might fire back at Cristina for spreading rumors about her personal life, to which Cristina might reply, "You're only acting this way because you're jealous of me. I don't have to deal with the same problems you do."

## Incessant Need to be Right

We all know when to step down and back off, especially if we're wrong. If you happen to stumble upon a narcissist, though, they might insist on being right even when they're explicitly mistaken. It doesn't matter if the topic of debate is unimportant or trivial, these people will refuse to accept defeat in all of its forms.

Narcissists will showcase aggression when trying to prove a point and will muscle you into agreeing to what they say to avoid being made to look 'wrong.' Even with all the facts laid out in front of them, they will continue to hold their ground. If all else fails, they might end the conversation with a cold, "Whatever you say. What I know is that this is the truth."

## Revels in Being Elite

Narcissists fancy themselves to be better than most, and that gives them the status of an elite. They'll strive to rub elbows with the high, the mighty, the rich, and the famous in order to be considered one of those folks. That's why they often end up in leadership roles because they're assertive, aggressive, and incredibly confident in themselves.

In a lot of ways, it does them good because they often have fulfilling careers and high paying jobs. On the downside, they might have stepped on a few people to get there, without feeling sorry for the damage they dealt.

During conversation, narcissists might keep drawing attention to certain status symbols that exude their elite status. New cars, a new home, children in prestigious, private schools, close ties with successful people, and just about anything else that might make you think, "Wow, this guy is minted!"

## A Fault-Free Existence

Have you ever tried to blame a narcissist for a problem or a bad outcome? Consider yourself lucky for making it out alive. These people refuse to accept the blame for anything, because, well, 'they're always right.'

As a result, you'll notice that most bad things that happen in their lives are always pinned on others around them. They're quick to blame even the closest family and friends for all the things that go wrong but will throw a fit and fight anyone who tries to do the same to them.

Even when their narcissistic ways put their relationships in hot water, they'll choose to simply toss that person out of their lives in order to avoid having to claim defeat. That's just how they roll.

## People are Dispensable

Doesn't matter who you are – friend, family, husband, children. Everyone is dispensable to a narcissist. These people have no problem cutting ties and throwing people away if that means they get to stand their ground and maintain their image.

In some families, a narcissistic parent might completely cut out a child if he or she refuses to follow their parent's desires. 'Disobedient' children that make the parent 'look bad' are liabilities to their image and threaten to destroy the narcissist's exterior shell of perfection.

So, to prevent family and friends from branding the narcissist as an ineffective parent, she will likely cut off the child and perhaps make up a story to wash her hands and put the blame on her estranged kid.

This is common in families with narcissistic parents because they see their children as 'extensions' of themselves. That said, they demand that their children act a certain way in order to maintain their clean, wholesome, and admirable image. Anyone who steps out of line threatens that and is thus unworthy of being part of the family of 'elites.'

## A Need to Control

Since they're 'right about everything,' isn't it only appropriate for them to take the reins on almost every situation around them, whether or not it's actually their place to call the shots? In the example of Jocelyn and Angela, this is a narcissistic quality that's made easy to perceive.

Narcissists need to control everything around them because they feel that they're better equipped to handle any and every situation. They'll call in a plumber just to take the tools and get the job done themselves. They'll dictate the directions from the backseat because the driver is just a little too dense for their liking. They'll take on any chore or task even if they don't want to just to prove that they can.

In families, a narcissistic parent will control anything that their child does or is, from the way they dress, to their academic performance, to the way they should interact with others around them. Narcissists will put severe limitations on freedom in the guise of protection, just because they feel unsettled when their child isn't within view for them to control.

Friendships with narcissists might also feel quite odd. For starters, a narcissist might control your feelings about certain people, especially if those individuals are the ones they don't like. They'll control how you feel, and they'll gaslight you to make you feel doubtful of things that you initially believed.

## The Narcissist Effect

Over time, you'll start to question your friend as the reality of their personality might start to show through the cracks. They're no longer perfect, and they might seem unreasonable, difficult, and at times, even toxic to be around, which they are. But because of your initial concept of them, you might find it difficult to come to terms with the reality.

What's more, you've already seen what happens to people who might get on their bad side. Because most of your friends and family are theirs as well, you might feel compelled to avoid confrontation in order to protect your image from their onslaught and aggression.

Generally, you should want to stay away from narcissists at all costs because it's hard to get out of their web once you're intertwined. So, keeping these markers in mind when facing new people can help you determine narcissistic tendencies before you're in too deep.

But what about the people that you can't choose? What about those who have been in your life for a while, but you've only just now realized are narcissists? How do you deal with them and is it possible to keep them in your life without ruining your relationships and your reputation?

# Chapter 2

# Causes Of Toxic/Negative Behavior

There are many reasons why you can attract toxic relationships but let me tell you the ugly truth first—no one is safe. Whether you are of good character or you are toxic yourself, toxic relationships are bound to be around you, circling like eagles eyeing a prey on the ground. It is a different question, however, if you allow them to come into your life and stay. In brief and precise words, I have explained the various reasons why you attract toxic relationships in paragraphs to follow.

Low Self-Esteem

Try to score your self-esteem. If you have any doubt at all, then you fit the profile of a person who will certainly fall prey to toxic relationships. If you doubt your self-worth and value, then you will welcome and give deference to anyone who seems to reinforce your suspicions and turn them into a conviction. Any of the teammates on Ridley's team could be like this, doubting their self-worth because they believe there is someone who is worth way much more than they are worth, and they bow to this person.

## Victim of Bullies

Another reason you can fall prey to toxic relationships, especially the manipulative and aggressive types, is if you have been a victim of bullies and have never stood up against their oppression. Your mentality is one of immediate submission to a force you think is greater than yours. The manipulative toxic person preys on you because he sees a weakness in you, the longing for approval, for recognition from others. He flatters you into doing his bidding. The aggressive, toxic person finds you a willing prey because you have the tendency never to stand up for yourself, never to challenge the dominance of others over you.

## Excessive Caring

If you are the type of person who cares very much about others and little about yourself, you are bound to keep the company of toxic relationships. The reason is simple: in caring too much for others, you become incredibly willing to please others and not to annoy them. You are ready to give up your seat to someone who even asks rudely for it. You are ready to inconvenience yourself for the benefit of others whose approval you seek. You are a fertile ground on which the seeds of toxicity will grow, and so the toxic relationships plant. When they harvest, you will be lucky to still have your life intact.

Good Upbringing

If you had a good upbringing, you might also fall prey to toxic relationships. That is strange, right? I will explain it. Recall that the causes of toxicity are all traced to poor upbringing of one kind or another. So, if you are lucky enough not to have been raised by parents who excessively pampered you, or by parents who scolded you all the time, or if your parents showed you adequate love and attention while you were growing up, then you have everything the toxic person was denied. You radiate a balance of character, a work of excellence, which the toxic person envies and would like to destroy. How is it possible, he asks, that you are naturally not interested in smoking crack or drinking too much? To the toxic person, this is an abomination, and he is determined to rid you of it. He only rests after he sees you indulging in what he indulges in.

You Are Toxic, Too?

Birds of a feather flock together, they say. This is very true in the case of toxicity. Toxic relationships are attracted to one another. If you are the type of person who is willing to do anything to please another, to gain their approval and retain their attention on you and you alone, then there is toxicity in you, too. You will do anything to get what you want—that approval—and manipulating others is just one of the tricks in your bag. Another prominent one is throwing emotional tantrums. Someone like you will attract the narcissist or the nerdy toxic person who is self-centered. The narcissist's desire to be adored, glorified, and even worshipped by others plays into and fits your willingness to gratify others at all costs.

Now, tell me, is anyone safe from the tentacles of toxic relationships? If this is true, then you need to be able to identify the toxic relationships in your life. How do you do this? By asking them if they are toxic? By asking them to fill out a questionnaire? Is there a simple, easy way to identify toxic relationships, a method devoid of all the complexities a psychologist might employ?

# Chapter 3

## Setting Boundaries

There are relationships we get into that offer us numerous benefits. They help us improve and ensure we are better than we were before the relationship. However, some relationships have the opposite effect. They make us lose our self-worth as individuals and change us into worse people than we were when we got into the relationship.

These sorts of partners tend to hurt you purposely or unknowingly until you begin to doubt everything. Many toxic individuals who could be your spouse, co-worker, or friend continue to manipulate you till you believe you are responsible for all the problems they are dealing with. These sorts of individuals deplete and drain all of your energy.

Regardless of where you find yourself, you do not want to be in a toxic relationship with anyone. For this reason, you need to learn to recognize a toxic relationship, and we will be teaching you how in this chapter. But first, why is it important to learn how to spot a toxic relationship?

# Why Is It Vital to Learn How to Recognize a Toxic Relationship?

In relationships, the parties involved are expected to be of help to one another when things are not so rosy without having any expectation of a returned favor. You're supposed to help each other in times of need. When a lot of people hear the word "relationship," what comes to their minds is a romantic relationship involving two members of the opposite sex. Although very widespread, this is not precise. This is because any two individuals can be involved in a relationship, and toxic relationships do not have to be between people involved romantically.

Humans flourish when they have company and feel bad when alone. When one is in a toxic relationship, such a person might battle with inner conflicts which might result in depression, anxiety, or anger. It is vital that you can spot signs of a toxic relationship, as well as toxic individuals. This way, you can avoid unwanted emotional traumas. Below, we will be delving into a few signs of a toxic relationship.

You have Become Isolated

If you have started staying away from your friends and loved ones because of your relationship, then it is a red flag. If it seems your partner is discouraging you from spending time with people you love, suddenly your relationship has become toxic. This is a primary technique used by narcissists who have the aim of completely dominating you.

Isolation is usually not apparent. The toxic partner does it subtly via different tactics. These could range from taking charge of the events or activities the other partner takes part in, always calling to "check up" on them, or requesting that their partner stops other personal activities because their relationship takes priority.

Another strategy used by the toxic partner to isolate the victim is via financial abuse. Here, the toxic partner takes complete charge of how the other partner spends cash or earns it. A partner who uses this technique may request that you stop your job or get a new one because it is not giving you enough time to focus on your relationship. In the end, you may start to depend on the partner for financial assistance, which is their goal.

A healthy relationship consists of 2 mature individuals. As adults, you do not need to request permission from your partners when trying to do basic things. Compromise is essential in relationships, and it is vital to think of your partner when making massive life decisions, such as having to undergo extensive surgery or buy a new house. However, if it feels like you have to seek permission before doing minor things like spending time with friends or going to the store, or you appear to be uncomfortable when making fundamental decisions without your partner, it could show that there is something wrong and a clear sign you are in a toxic relationship.

Through the use of isolation as a means of cutting you off from your family and others around you, the toxic partner gets more control. Isolation can also be used in creating a vacuum in the relationship for the toxic partner to engage in other harmful and destructive behaviors. Eventually, victims may feel that they have no one to confide in about their experiences. This leaves the victim without a support system during perilous times.

If you observe all of these in your relationship, then it is a clear sign that you are dealing with a toxic relationship.

Asymmetric Relationship

Asymmetric relationships occur when one of the two partners in a romantic relationship has an excessively dominant role. In essence, one of the partners is more devoted to the relationship than the other partner.

Researchers grounded this concept on a theory established by sociologist Willard Waller. The theory was known as the "Principle of Least Interest." This theory connotes that the individual with a lower amount of interest in the relationship has a higher level of control. This is why many individuals urge themselves to act cool in social situations. It is also why many people take excess time in responding to texts even though they have an interest in the person (Stanley et al., 2018).

In a more recent study, researchers decided to try out this theory in romantic relationships. This was done to determine the kind of partners who keep the most control in relationships. Below are a few things they observed, which may indicate that you are in an asymmetric relationship (Stanley et al., 2018):

- Your partner believes that there are numerous fish in the sea.
- Your partner has issues getting attached and opening up to others.
- They have numerous exes.
- If your partner has cheated on you or does so continuously.

If you have observed that your partner does any or all of the following, then you may be dealing with an asymmetric relationship, which makes it a toxic one.

Other ways your relationship could be asymmetric include:

You are Obsessively Dependent

Codependency is categorized as a relationship where two individuals become so attached and invested in each other that they are no longer able to function separately. In this situation, the identity, happiness, and mood are determined by one of the partners. In these sort of relationships, one person has more dominance over the other. What's more, this individual gets a feeling of fulfillment from controlling the other partner and how they live. In this case, this is the toxic partner.

Dependence on someone you love and hope to spend the rest of your life with is not generally a bad thing. However, when you get obsessively dependent on your partner, who starts to show signs of control, this may be a problem. Being controlled by your partner and being excessively dependent on them don't go without one another. A toxic or controlling partner usually makes you dependent on them so you can help them satisfy their requirements. They may manipulate you until your entire life revolves around them, which gives them more control over you.

You need to remember that being excessively dependent on another individual is not due to love, but fear. When a toxic partner makes you responsible for them staying happy, their constant requirement to be validated begins to seem like an addiction. Your partner starts to control you, and it transforms into emotional dependency because you don't want to lose your partner. Being excessively dependent on your partner can lead you to totally let go of your identity to make your partner happy. Besides, your self-esteem may be centered on the relationship without your knowledge. If your relationship has started to feel this way, then it may have become a toxic one. If you are not sure about this, below are some of the general signs that can help you determine if your relationship is an emotionally dependent toxic relationship:

- You find it hard to make any decisions without your partner.
- You have trouble pointing out your feelings.
- You have low self-esteem and don't trust your judgment.
- You are scared of being abandoned and desire a constant need for approval
- You have problems expressing yourself in your relationship.

Individuals who are excessively dependent on others have a higher likelihood of transforming even healthy relationships into toxic ones. If you notice yourself portraying any of the symptoms listed above, then this is a major sign of a toxic relationship.

They Blackmail You

Emotional blackmail is an elaborate means of manipulation where individuals we are close to dish out threats to us because we failed to do their bidding. This is a prevalent strategy used by toxic partners. Many toxic partners who are apt at emotional blackmail understand the value we place on the relationships we have with them. They know your darkest secrets and know your weaknesses, which are typically not a bad thing in a healthy relationship. However, in the hands of a toxic partner, this can be very dangerous. If you observe that your partner is hurting and manipulating you as a means of punishing you, then it is a clear sign that you are in a toxic relationship.

There are many strategies used by the toxic partner to blackmail you emotionally. All of these are done to make you do their biddings. They include:

Capitalizing on your Fears

Fear is a feeling which keeps us safe from jeopardy. However, a toxic partner can take advantage of this feeling of fear to make you do their bidding. Below are the kinds of worries these toxic partners capitalize on to manipulate you:

- Fear of being abandoned
- Fear of getting others upset
- Fear of being abandoned
- Fear of confrontation
- Fear for your safety

Capitalizing on your Sense of Obligation

A toxic partner can make you feel obligated so they can do what they want. To achieve this, they use various strategies to make you feel bad about yourself if you don't carry out your obligations. For instance; if your partner requests that you do something you are uncomfortable with, and they remind you of all the times they went out of their way for you or tell you they would have done the same for you. Regardless of the way they go about it, you will feel a sense of duty to do their bidding, even if it is not your desire.

Guilt-Tripping you

Many toxic partners use your guilt to punish you. If you fail to do your obligations, they can use your guilt until you feel bad about yourself and do what they want.

If you have ever been blackmailed by your partner using any of the following methods, then you may be in a toxic relationship.

# Chapter 4

## Moving On

Now that we have already discussed what difficult behavior is, and the classically different types of person, let us now go to a serious and a very usual circumstance and event in that happens in any workplace: Conflict. Put it in simple words, it can be defined as direct opposition between ideas or interests. It arises when a person disagrees to the other person's point of views or beliefs.

In any conflict situation there would always be two important factors to be considered. The objective point in which the parties do not agree on and the emotions or personal perceptions that goes along the situation. Plainly speaking, you have to be aware that in dealing with conflicts in the office you must set aside the second factor and focus on the objective facts in which the situation is supposed to be based on.

According to Blaine Donais, author of Workplaces That Work published by Canada Law Book, the successful administration of work environment conflict obliges a comprehension of the nature and wellsprings of conflict in the work environment. It happens when there is a view of contrary point of views between work environment members. This ought to be recognized from arguments. They are simply a by-result of conflict. They are the outward explanation of it. Run of the mill arguments come as formal court cases, grievances, contentions, dangers and counter dangers and so forth. Conflict can exist without arguments, however it doesn't exist without conflict. In any case, this conflict may not be easily noticed. Much of it exists in every working environment without transforming into arguments.

For us to deeply understand workplace conflict we first must know its sources. Though in this book we would be mostly dealing with people conflicts these could help you have a better understanding of organizational setup which includes these conflict sources that includes interpersonal, change related, external factors and organizational.

1. Interpersonal

Interpersonal conflict is the most apparent form of conflict in the workplace. It is not that difficult enough for you to be aware of the results of rumors, gossips and sometimes even office politics. Moreover, language and personality styles may often clash, resulting into a great deal of conflict. There are also strong racial and ethno-cultural sources of conflict as well as gender ones. These scenarios may lead to charges of harassment and judgment or at least the feeling that such things actually prevail. People also often bring their problems from home into the workplace resulting to further conflict. Another underlying reason for regarding workplace conflict can also be found in changing thoughts regarding individual achievements. The solid commute for business related accomplishment in a few members could cause conflict with members who don't underline business related achievement in their lives.

To help you reveal some sources of conflict, you may use personality testing instruments Personality Dynamics Profiles, Thomas-Kilman, FIRO-B and the very popular Myers-Briggs. Moreover there are other instruments you may use like forming of focus groups, conducting scheduled interviews and confidential surveys.

2.  Change related (Trends)

Nowadays the workplace has increased noticeably the levels of stress and conflict due to many changes including critical downsizing and change of management. Other changes also include technological advancements and different work methodologies. Many professional are also aware of the constant reorganization that also leads to conflict. In relation to this reorganization, non-profit organizations sometimes find it necessary to shift their other work responsibilities to other related organizations. Those people who specialize in analyzing workplace behaviors of people must check the history of the organization going back as far as ten years to know the level of churn that has already occurred. Generally, the greater and recent the change is, the more significant the conflict will be expected.

3.  External Factors

These factors could be sum up to evolving markets, effects of approving free trade amongst countries, foreign and domestic competition, and recession that also results to economic pressures. Conflict emerges with customers and suppliers effecting client administration and conveyance of products. Additionally, non-profit organizations specifically could face political pressures and demands form particular vested parties. Government change may have a great impact on every organization may it be public or not. Those organizations dependent on government funding could change their funding levels dramatically. Public philosophies could also have an effect on the system of treating employees and also on the way those who are in the higher management view them upon.

To search for outer elements of conflict, have an audit of the connections between the subject association and different associations. Organizations or government offices that have steady associations with outsiders will discover this to be a significant source of conflict for workplace members.

4.  Organizational

There are various sources of conflict on this one. Those identifying with hierarchy and the lack of ability to resolve contradicting interests are very prevalent in many work environments. Due to power differences labor and employee tensions are heightened. The differences in management and leadership styles between departments can also be a source of conflict. It could also include seniority, pay balance and work style conflict. This type of dissonance may arise over the dissemination of responsibilities, resource allocation, types of work and benefits, distinctive levels of resistance for risk taking, and changing perspectives on responsibility. What's more, conflict can emerge where there are seen or genuine contrasts in treatment between divisions or gatherings of representatives.

A careful survey of the work environment is recommended for such sources of conflict. Again reviews, meetings and focus groups can help uncover these sources. Furthermore, organizational sources can be anticipated based upon best practices from comparable associations. All associations experience such conflict. Much can be found out from the lessons of comparative associations who have made an investigation of these sources of conflict.

# Chapter 5

## Acceptance

We all find manipulating other people's minds unethical. This is because we consider it as playing with people's feelings as well as thoughts and emotions in order for it to benefit us alone. That is considered a very selfish move. Manipulators know how to play their cards well. They will make sure that they use all the available techniques to manipulate the targeted people. Whether manipulation is unethical or not mostly depends on an individual. This is because we are the ones with the final decision as to whether we should allow them to manipulate us or not.

One is therefore required to evaluate themselves every often in order for them to ensure that they have the required skills for them to be able to avoid manipulators. In this chapter, I am going to discuss some of the many manipulation techniques that one can use to manipulate, persuade and influence people.

Fear and Relief Technique

Fear and relief is a technique that is said to be very efficient when it comes to playing with other people's emotions. A manipulator is only required to instill some fear on an individual, which immediately makes them vulnerable. At the time when they are vulnerable, the manipulator does anything they want in their favor. The manipulator manipulates the individual at this point since they know that the victim will do anything to get out of the fearful situation.

The only challenge that the manipulator might encounter when using this technique is identifying the things that make them fear. They will, therefore, need to keep fearful situations to the every now and then until when they will identify it. The manipulators succeed in this situation since most people hate situations that make them fear. They would anything to make sure that they get out of the situation.

An example of how this technique is used is when the media wants to keep its viewers following the channel. They will put up a juicy headline, which will keep the viewers glued on the screen waiting for it. The reporter will then keep reporting that they need to keep watching the program in order for them to get the juicy news. Everyone will keep watching in the hope that the program will still come.

With fear and relief techniques, the manipulator is expected to instill fear until when they see that the manipulator is about to give up. It is at this point that they will be able to relieve them of the pressure that they are going through which makes them less stressful. The fearful situation that they have been through makes them obey the manipulator's orders anytime they give them since they would not want to go back to the situation they were in before.

## Guilty Approach Technique

Through the guilty approach technique, the manipulator makes their prey guilty in order for them to be able to manipulate them. They will make sure that they blame them for things they did not do. One will want to compensate the manipulator without the knowledge that they will are about to be manipulated. A manipulator has to however make sure that their target is someone who is prone to feeling guilty.

Once you make the person guilty, you will be able to swing them in any direction since they are willing to do anything to make sure that you forget the things that they did to you. It works so perfectly since according to the victim, they will compensate for the moments that they were not nice to you but for the manipulator, it will be time to use them for their selfish gain. The guilt approach technique, therefore, works so well when one wants to influence other people since the victim will be feeling an obligation to make it up to you for the trouble they caused you. Little do they know that the manipulator was waiting for such a moment to strike?

## Playing the Victim

This type of technique is somehow similar to the guilty approach technique. Playing the victim may however work against you if not careful when implementing it. You would be required to ensure that you do not overuse it. The trick is normally to ensure that you make the targeted person feel bad about a given situation. You will be required to ensure that the person actually made the mistake but for you, playing the victim shall be an exaggeration. The victim will feel bad about it and will want to compensate it by doing something different for you. They will, therefore, be nice to you, which will help the manipulator to use them to achieve her goals.

Love Bombing Technique

We all like it when we feel loved by the people around us. We will all appreciate it when the people around us make us feel appreciated and loved. That is why manipulators use love and attention to manipulate people.

This technique is mostly used for the purposes of manipulating people emotionally. A manipulator will mostly give a lot of attention to their targeted individual. They will show them a lot of affection, which would make them, not suspect anything from the manipulator. By doing this, they will be setting up a trap for them. They will be laying the ground, which they will use for their manipulation purposes. When the right time comes, they are able to easily execute their plan. This means that by the time they realize that you are manipulating them; they will have already been influenced to a place of no return.

Bribery Technique

This technique is said to work like a charm. This is because you will reward someone out of nowhere and they will automatically want to return the favor in a different way. It is an easy job since you are only required to find out what your victim needs and you get them exactly that. You will only be expected to look as genuine as possible. This will make the person really happy such that if you ever mention that you need anything, they will not hesitate to get it for you. By doing this, you will be able to make demands from them as many times as possible without them noticing that you are manipulating them. Through this technique, you will have influenced people to your system, which they may find it difficult to exit.

Becoming a Good Listener

A manipulator knows that people need good listeners in their lives. A good listener earns people's trust so easily. This is because they will come out as being very caring and concerned. This makes the victim trust them completely. A manipulator cannot manipulate people before gaining their trust. Once you have their trust, it will be very easy to manipulate them. You will only be required to discuss with them a few things that you may be going through and without even questioning, they will reciprocate for it since you were there for them before. Through the trust, the manipulator will be able to manipulate them for a long time without the victim noticing.

In as much as a manipulator uses these skills to manipulate, persuade and influence people, they all need to be good in some skills. Some of the skills have been discussed below.

- They need to have excellent verbal communication skills. No one will listen to someone who cannot communicate clearly. You would need to be able to express yourself well if at all you want people to listen to you. Most manipulators have mastered this skill very well which helps them to prey on people without them noticing. When one is good in communication, they are able to easily prey on the victims with the language that they understand. The victims will, therefore, understand the manipulator very well and follow all the instructions given without knowing that they are in the trap of being manipulated.

- For a manipulator to be able to manipulate and persuade people, they should look good before them. Your way of dressing and the way you present yourself tells a lot about you. People will only take you seriously when you look good. You will be able to earn their trust easily. People are normally impressed by people who dress nicely, who are well kept and also who have manners. They will easily like them and listen to them and in the process trust them. Once trust kicks in, the manipulators are able to easily persuade them as well as influence them in the direction that they want.

- When you are conversant about psychology, you will be able to read people's minds. You will be able to know how they feel, how they will react to certain things and also their mood. Knowing all this will be of great help in ensuring that you use their weaknesses to your advantage. You will be able to manipulate them without their knowledge.

# Chapter 6

## The Roots Of Suffering

The chapter was keen enough to take us through the facets of manipulation. This chapter, however, focuses its radar on the art of persuasion. Before we indulge further into the major facets of persuasion, we will first have to comprehend the meaning of persuasion. Persuasion refers to the psychological influence which affects the choice that an individual ought to make. With persuasion, an individual is often inclined to make you buy his or her school of thought in a bid to change your thought process. In order for one to effectively achieve persuasion, there are a number of things that need to be put in mind. When we are able to go beyond the natural human framework and get a grasp of what moves others, then you are in a position to achieve effective persuasion. This is because you are aware of the pressure points and how best to manipulate them.

When exploiting the art of persuasion, there are various pointers that can come in handy. These are:

Mimicking

As human beings of reason, we tend to vary from one individual to another. The diversity of this is what makes us appear in the discrepancy of others. Owing to this particular fact, you will find that as individuals, we are more drawn to be warm and welcoming to those people who exhibit the same characteristics as us. It could be a physical trait or just the way an individual carries themselves out. This type of technique is said to elicit positive feelings that go a mile when it comes to persuasion. When an individual has the feelings of liking towards someone, he or she is in a position to be swayed by your influence.

In a bid to elaborate on this particular type of technique, we are going to employ the use of this scenario. In the hotel industry, especially in the most advanced and high-end ones, you will find that the allocation of a waiter is dependent on the customer. High-end hotels in the industry have high customer feedback and thus they tend to treat their clients in a manner that suggests so. A client, for instance, would be allocated a particular type of waiter who matches their description. For instance, French waiters are renowned for their exquisite service. Putting the client first is at the top of the list when it comes to this particular field. Many professionals have succeeded in this area owing to the manner in which they treated clients. This is because of the clients re the main source of business. Putting the client into consideration goes a notch higher to even saying the exact words that the client has said. With this, they are able to gather that you have aptly decoded what they meant.

In order to accurately achieve this particular technique, an individual ought to do a number of things. First, he or she may consider doing in-depth research into the particular field of the question in order to see to it that what is required of them is met. Before you are able to achieve persuasion by the use of this technique, one ought to be well versed with the individual that he or she ought to persuade. This type of expertise should be keen enough to make sure that it elicits major points that may come in handy during the process of persuasion.

Social Proof

When it comes to persuasion, social proof has repeatedly proven its dominance. Before we go deeper into the technique, we first need to gather the meaning of social proof. Social proof refers to the process by which an individual's feelings and thought process are affected by the way other people have reacted to the same issue. When it comes to social influence. An individual who is the persuader, draw his or her basis from the acts that others have engaged in time and again. It could be the norm. With human beings, the danger that occurs is the feeling of wanting to be associated with a group of people. Human beings want to accrue a sense of belonging either to a group of people or to a particular act and this is what puts them at a higher risk of being influenced easily.

Employing social proof when persuading an individual will mean that you have a basis of a norm that has been used repeatedly by the people whom we consider to be in the same class. This basis must be something that most people engage in and not a few numbers. Take, for instance, there are newbies in the estate who are looking for service providers. This newbie would first be inclined to know what other people in the estate are using. Although they might not settle on the same option as the rest of the estate, this will be somewhat a buildup on to what choice they may choose to settle upon. Rather they may end up embracing what others have used. With this technique, the trick lies whereby you ought to create a distinction in the manner in which an individual sees himself or herself as per against others. You will only achieve persuasion by convincing this individual that the desired option is one that has been embraced by a large group of individuals.

Reciprocity

When it comes to this type of technique, one needs to understand that a good deed was done to another individual no matter how remote, tends to go a long way. From the wording of it, reciprocity refers to the process by which an individual is able to respond to a good deed by performing a good deed in return. With this type of technique, we will find that most people fail to notice at its onset not until you are obligated to return the favor. In the world today, it is almost as rare as the sun rising from the west as it is to find someone who will extend feelings of warmness and care towards you. Save the people whom we are closely related, we tend to feel differently when an individual who is not even in your circle of friendship extends warm-hearted feelings.

The feeling of obligation arises as a result of being extended a good deed by an individual. This is the result of being extended with feelings of warmness. At this point, you are in a position to persuade the individual in the manner that you wish. This is because he or she would be obliged to follow in the direction of the wind. It should be noted that this particular type of technique ought to be time cautious. This is because the implication of reciprocity does not last forever. There are limits to this timeline and one should be cautious enough to make sure that these limits are not exploited. With the passing of more time, it weakens the wave of reciprocity.

In order to achieve this particular type of technique, an individual ought to play in the tone of offers and obligations. If your offer is worth it, then it raises an obligation effect on the other hand. Thus creating a win situation.

Consistency and Commitment

This type of technique is wired on an already formed perception. An individual is in a position to settle on a particular choice. The choice that this individual picks would be pegged on him or her for as far as they go. From the wording of it, consistency and commitment refer to the fact that an individual is in a position to make a choice and stick to it with sheer determination and perseverance. When it comes to persuasion, not all techniques may work and you may find that you hit rock bottom once or twice in your venture. When this happens, it is not advisable to give up. Consistency is what builds our character in almost every facet in life. This type of technique is vast in a manner that cuts across various fields not limited to the field of education and business. The first approach to an individual for purposes of convincing them may or may not end up in a manner that you wish. The first approach is often one that is characterized by rejection and in some cases mental torture. The best way to respond to this type of instance is by not giving up. The second encounter of individuals who first rejected your idea will see to it that you have an audience who understands what you are talking about.

The talk of consistency and commitment is one that does not go down the throat easily. This is because these are the most subtle facets to embrace because they tend to take a toll on an individual. You can imagine getting rejected severally. In order to achieve commitment, an individual ought to operate in a manner that is relentless.

# Chapter 7

## Free At Last

## What Happens to Your Brain and How to Change

You cannot say an entire population is terrible just because a few people in it have done terrible things. There is a lot of hatred toward those with Borderline Personality Disorder, for example, and I am not here to further that.

The reason that I am incorporating so much about personality disorders is that when a person goes undiagnosed, or nobody confronts them on their problems, it leads to serious consequences. These words are only meant to inspire you to take action when you think somebody close to you is struggling. You are in no position to be throwing around disorders, however, so keep that in mind. This is only a reference tool to see if you spot any of the "psychological red flags" that would lead you to suggest the person seeks help.

There is also a huge difference between "sharing traits" with these disorders and actually having one. There is a reason that the DSM (the Diagnostic and Statistical Manual) is so black and white and puts serious limitations on diagnosing. Professionals in the medical field also have a strict policy against dealing with relatives or anybody close to them. You need to have an entirely unbiased opinion and at least four years of medial school behind you.

Now that the necessary pretext has been laid out, I think that it is a great time to start talking more in-depth about how, exactly, personality disorders are diagnosed. This goes for just about any type of mental illness, however. Even ones that are more "common," such as depression, normally have "high agitation" or "irritability" listed as a diagnostic criterion.

So, to the untrained eye, these disorders can look rather similar.

I am going to run down each one, as well as what the criteria are for diagnosing it. Earlier I talked about some of the "signs," as well as some stuff we already know about the disorders. This section is going to be far more scientific- but I will do my best to break it down so that it is easily digestible for you.

- Borderline Personality Disorder: This is a disorder that primarily affects the self-image that you hold. Those with Borderline tend to have long patterns of unstable relationships, high difficulty managing their emotions, and more. This is particularly hard to treat a disorder, but recovery rates are astoundingly high in many cases when CBT, or cognitive behavioral therapy, is used.

- The diagnostic criteria for Borderline Personality Disorder are fairly to the point. Unlike in some disorders, there is no specific number of months in which symptoms must happen. Instead, it is diagnosed based on the noted effects in the person's life as they grow into adulthood.

- The criteria are as follow:
- Using any means necessary to avoid abandonment, whether real or perceived
- Clear patterns of consistently unstable, and often intense, relationships
- These relationships will be marked by alternations between idealization and devaluation
- Having poor self-image and no real idea of "who" they are
- Showing signs of high impulsivity in relation to self-destructive behavior
- Frequent threats of suicide and self-harming behavior
- Extreme mood swings from one moment to the next
- Feeling chronically "empty" inside
- Poor control of temper
- Disassociation related to stress to the point of paranoia

- There are several different "self-destructive" behaviors that can be listed. Promiscuity, high spending, and excessive drinking are three ways in which this behavior can be engaged.

- Narcissistic Personality Disorder: This is a disorder that is mainly characterized by the excessive need for admiration and attention. Oftentimes, there will be little reason as to why this person "deserves" the praise that they seek. It is also notable that they will have a grandiose sense of self with a strong lack of empathy.

- Again, this is not a disorder that can be diagnosed by anybody other than a professional who specializes in the disorder. There is also a lot of work that people with this disorder need to put in before they improve. Oftentimes they will not show up to therapy because of their narcissism. Instead, they end up going for something unrelated and end up being referred to a specialist. It is normal for them to reject the diagnoses and refuse to engage with the process of recovery, as well.

- The criteria are as follow:

- Having a self-image which is grandiose

- Greatly exaggerating accomplishments or other talents

- Requires special treatment without reason

- Preoccupation with fantasies surrounding recognition for their brilliance, unlimited success, and other similar ideals

- Exceedingly high sense of being entitled

- Exploits and manipulates all of those around them as a means to their ends

- Very low levels of empathy

- Frail self-esteem and lack of confidence

- Those who suffer from Narcissistic Personality disorder can, absolutely, recover. The question is not if they can, it is whether or not they want to. You will most likely find that they are entirely unwilling to take accountability.

- It is important to note, however, that this more so due to having to accept the damage they have dealt with. Accepting that means processing it and realizing that they have left a trail of wreckage behind them. The most dangerous time for a person being treated for NPD is this phase. Accepting what you have done, and actively developing the empathy to understand why it was wrong, is enough to make anybody suicidal.

- Anti-Social Personality Disorder: Perhaps the most often talked about, Anti-Social Personality Disorder is often also misunderstood. Most people use the words "Sociopath" and "Psychopath" in place of the disorder's actual name. If you take nothing else from this section, take away the idea that neither of those words is a disorder. In fact, they are only used to describe behavior which fits into different disorders diagnostic criteria.

- Those who have ASPD lack empathy entirely. As a result, they will have a long record of aggressive or violent behavior. They will also, as a general rule, have numerous run-ins with law enforcement and criminal history. Their inability to feel empathy translates into complete and utter interpersonal chaos.

- Understand that there are several different subtypes for this disorder. All of them are entirely dangerous. Part of the criteria for it says as much, as it turns out. I think that this will make more sense if I just jump into that part of it, however.

- The criteria are as follow:

- Refusal to obey laws, both social and legal, and engaging in unlawful behavior as a result

- Repeated patterns of lying, using falsified names, engaging in con artist behavior, and exploiting others for profit or pleasure

- Inability to plan for the future

- High levels of aggression and poor temper control

- Entirely disregards the safety of others or self

- Irresponsible behavior which leads to an inability to meet financial obligations or inability to hold down a job at all

- Inability to feel remorse as a result of their actions

- Please note that you must be at least 18 before this disorder can be diagnosed. Part of personality disorders is that before our brains finish developing, our personality is fairly fluid. Early intervention at the onset of symptoms goes a long way in putting the person on a correct path before they are too far gone.

Remember, these are extreme disorders that cause extreme behavior. While you may feel as though a toxic person in your life exhibits these behaviors, it may just be that they are "narcissistic" in personality, but do not have a disordered personality.

On the other hand, you may also be experiencing a toxic relationship with somebody who has been formally diagnosed.

If you know that the person has the disorder, and has not just self-diagnosed themselves, this information is vital. On that note, this is something else you should look for as a red flag for toxicity. Somebody glamorizing personality disorders and claiming to have one, while having never been formally diagnosed, has become more and more popular. This is not necessarily a sign of a personality disorder, however.

In most cases, these are people who are highly toxic. They do not have an understanding of the extremity with which those who actually have personality disorders act. Many of these types of people are doing so for attention and fail to grasp the severity of the situation. This type of person is, absolutely, a red flag unto themselves. I recommend steering clear of anybody who makes light of mental illness in general, but especially those glamorizing it.

Now, I think it is important that I go over the science behind the personality types, as well. Earlier I went over them in a brief way and spoke about how they related to the topic at hand. Now I am going to get a little bit deeper into them, and why they are so great at classifying people. Our brains work in mysterious ways, but hopefully, yours will feel less mysterious after this!

INFJ

- What is the Myers Briggs Type Indicator (MBTI)?: This is a fantastic tool created by two women after thoroughly studying the work of Carl Jung. His theory of personality types is what inspired them to develop this system of identification. While neither were "scientists," they were absolute experts on interpersonal systems and the science of people.

- This is now one of the most commonly used methods of psychological evaluation. Many businesses have incorporated it into their offices in order to better understand employees. Many hold it in the highest of esteems, and it has proven time and time again to be highly effective.

- The Characterization of INFJs: Did you know that this is the rarest of all the personality types in the MBTI? INFJs are a quirky bunch and highly dedicated to the world around them. They tend to be driven to enact change and help the world become a better place. INFJs are generally predisposed to burning out because of their need to always be furthering their ideals.

- You will also find that INFJs are incredibly people-oriented. They want to spend time making sure the world around them is actively becoming a better place. While less than 1% of the population shares this personality type, they tend to be the people who leave the biggest marks on the world around them.

- Why this Type is Predisposed: As you can imagine, those who fall into the INFJ category are idealists. They often want to sympathize with others as much as possible and can be taken advantage of as a result. Since they are also predisposed to burning out, toxic relationships can take an extra toll on them. They do not want to "give up" on the person with who they are having trouble. Instead, they want to help them.

- This creates a toxic cycle in which the INFJ is constantly pulled back into the toxic relationship. They cannot "get away" from the person because they know that they can somehow help them. "Giving up" is not a phrase in the vocabulary of many INFJs, especially those who are devoted to the toxic person in their life.

## Empathic

- What Makes People Empathic: This is a largely arguable question, with many entirely undecided on the answer. Scientists and laymen alike have been wondering for years what, exactly, empathy is. In fact, we really do not understand how it develops, either. Neuropsychology is a brand-new field, and because of that we are still in the infancy of the discoveries ahead. There are a few commonly held beliefs on the matter, however. Most of our evidence shows that empathy is largely learned.

- This is why early trauma and abuse can cause a person to develop low empathy. You must be taught by those around you to display emotional regard for others. It is part of learning to "share" and how to get along with others. When a person is not exposed to these ideas early on, it can create a seeming inability to feel empathy.

- Most of the normal play you see children engage in will cultivate empathy, as well. Play is important not only for children but also for adults. It helps us build understanding, work with others, and more. Building your emotional intelligence and empathy does not have to be difficult. That leads us to our next topic!

- Emotional Intelligence: There are several ways in which you can build your emotional intelligence. Most of them are not very difficult, too. It is important to consistently work towards understanding those around us. This is not just good for empathizing- it is good for protecting ourselves. Being able to spot red flags early because you have a great understanding of people is something that you need to hone. This will help you in all aspects of your life.

- Emotional intelligence refers to your ability to understand the emotions of others. It is kind of like the idea of "standard" intelligence. While standard intelligence is based on the ability to recognize patterns and solve problems, emotional intelligence is based on your ability to read people and understand interpersonal situations.

- I will be going over several different methods of building emotional intelligence later on in the book.

## Highly Sensitive

- What Constitutes "Highly Sensitive": This is a tricky one since all of us, at one point or another, could be classified as "highly sensitive." I suppose the best way to look at it is to understand the frequency of these scenarios. By that, I mean how often you feel like others do not like you, or how easily you cry. Timid, meek people tend to be highly sensitive and highly reliant on others for reassurance.

- Those who are highly sensitive do not act with aggression or lash out as a result of others inspiring these feelings within them. Instead, they tend to fall victim to depression or similar mindsets. Highly sensitive people are those who cry frequently without much prompting. If you cry every time you see a video of a cute animal, for example, you are definitely highly sensitive.

- The problem with this is that those who are highly sensitive need partners who validate and uplift them. There is nothing wrong with having incredibly high empathy- and that is, generally, what highly sensitive people have.

- Some People are Predisposed: There are two sides to every coin. Many people who did not receive enough attention or love as children end up being highly sensitive. Neglect and abuse can cause this, as it oftentimes will cause people to be overly empathetic instead of lacking empathy. That is part of why neuroscience is so complicated- we really do not understand why some people go to one extreme, while others go the exact another way.

- Having strict or overbearing parents can cause heightened sensitivity, as well. And, of course, some people are just born the way that they are.

- Overcoming High Sensitivity: Becoming more aware of yourself is the best way to begin overcoming a highly sensitive personality. You also need to begin engaging in confidence-building activities and exercises. There are several ways to do this, and most of them are incredibly easy. I will go over this far more in-depth later on in the book. For now, just understand that you can, in fact, rewire your brain. You do not have to be subject to the directions in which your brain pushes you.

- In order to overcome being highly sensitive, you need to push yourself to take part in challenging activities. There are so many things out there to help you, such as mindfulness or self-defense. High sensitivity is something many people struggle with.

## Codependents

- How Codependency Forms: There are many ways in which a codependent relationship can form. One of the largest is that one of the partners begins to look for validation from the other in a way that is entirely inappropriate. Codependency generally happens if the two partners are on "different playing fields," so to speak. What I mean by this is that if one is significantly further ahead in life than the other, there is a high risk for that partner to become codependent on the other.

- The problem with codependency is that it is not just about the one partner who has become codependent. The "co" is key here. Both partners will become intertwined in such a way that breaking free from the toxicity can be incredibly challenging.

- While it may begin with one of the partners leaning on the other, the fact of the matter is that at one point or another, both people become toxic. For example, the partner who is supporting the other may feel like they need to give that support because it makes them feel validated. They might also do it out of an innate sense of needing to "fix" others. And still, they may also just drive everybody around them away, and so a codependent relationship is the only one that can be successful for the person.

- Changes in the Brain: Like with any relationship, this has some serious consequences for your brain. This goes for all toxic relationships, however, and we'll get into that a little later in this chapter. In fact, it will be the rest of the chapter so we can get really down into it. I just want to preface the more complicated science with brief overviews.

- Essentially, you can become, quite literally, addicted to the other person.

- Overcoming Your Codependence: I want to impress upon you as much as possible that you do not need to stay in a codependent relationship. You also, however, do not need to reject relationships that you have. There is a chance to turn them around and choose a healthier way to intermingle with the person. It takes a lot of effort, and the setting of boundaries, but it is not impossible. The brain is constantly changing and making new connections. It is just about harnessing those connections!

I hope that was a much more thorough rundown on the science behind all of this information. My hope is that you have a solid foundation off of which to work. I highly encourage you to take the Myers-Briggs Type Indicator test if you have not already. It is a great way to figure out what kind of person you are and give you some more insight into how your mind works. There are a lot of people who encourage the usage of the MBTI in workplace environments, too, in order to soothe interpersonal clashing.

The MBTI can also help you understand how predisposed you may be too toxic relationships. Perhaps more importantly, it will, on top of that, key you in to whether or not you yourself are toxic.

There is a lot of blame which gets thrown around at victims caught up in toxic relationships. This is very unfortunate because, as science shows us, there is far more to it than just the "choice" to stay. If you are currently stuck in this kind of situation, know that my sympathy is with you. There is hope, and you are not a weak person. In fact, you are taking a very large, brave step by reading this book.

One of the biggest reasons people believe that people who stay in a toxic relationship is weak is that they do not understand the core of the matter. Just like with drug addiction, for example, it is hard to understand from the outside looking in. Having an addiction is no laughing matter. It can be almost as dangerous if that addiction is a person rather than a drug.

The brain makes connections constantly and is always rearranging to process and hold new information. This brain structure also largely mirrors those we surround ourselves with. This is why surrounding yourself with positive, forward-thinking people is so important. You need to make sure you are setting yourself up for success. This is always what comes first. Dealing with toxic relationships begins with dealing with yourself. I will talk about a bunch of exercises and such to help with just that later on in the book.

For now, let us get into what makes your brain tick and why it is so hard to detach yourself from people. Again, this is especially true for those who are stuck in abusive relationships. If you are one such person, I definitely recommend that you exit the relationship immediately. Abuse leaves a huge marker on your brain and can set you up for failure in the future. Nobody deserves to be in a relationship that is abusive. Seek help, because it is out there.

People stay for a variety of reasons. For example:

- Being underage (18 and under)
- Marriage
- Children
- Familiar relation
- Sharing a friend group

There are many more reasons- just as many as there are people! Each situation is unique and has its own set of challenges. Yours will, undoubtedly, be vastly different than any other person. You need to understand going into this that this will be generalized information. However, this is on purpose so that you can apply it to yourself as an individual.

In psychology, there is a concept known as "trauma bonding," and it is one of the reasons why people cannot see their abuser for what they are. Manipulative people have a way of using emotional abuse to get the same reaction out of their victims. Trauma, after all, does not just relate to physical violence. In fact, emotional trauma goes a long way in affecting the brain. You can easily develop PTSD related to emotional trauma.

You should note that PTSD from long-term emotional abuse is different than something which occurs due to a sudden, traumatic event. In fact, psychologists have begun to differentiate the two. C-PTSD, which is a complex post-trauma stress disorder, is a diagnosis all unto itself.

This happens in a few different steps. First, the abuser will have a "honeymoon" phase in which they treat the person incredibly well. Once this honeymoon phase is over, they begin to engage in abusive behaviors, which can range from emotional abuse to physical aggression.

Fear is what it all comes down to.

I am excited to share this knowledge with you, however, so let me get right into it.

# Chapter 8

―――― ❦❦❦❦ ――――

# The Toxic Termination Process (TTP)

We all think we've chosen wisely when it comes to those people who are our friends and who make our lives easier and more fun to experience. However, sometimes, despite our defenses, a toxic person manages their malignant manifestation.

If you keep your wits about you you'll soon detect them. Over a period of time their continuous backbiting and attrition becomes wearing. Or they do or say something so odious and reprehensible that it creates a tipping point, and you know that they deserve no place in your life.

So how do you deal with them? Once you've exhausted any attempts to negotiate with them, the straightforwardness of the approach given is breathtakingly elegant in its simplicity. It may require the qualities of determination, resolution and perseverance in how you play it out – qualities that are very useful to develop in any case and are replicable for other situations.

Consider it as a character-forming act.

Tell them you will have nothing further to do with them. Then ignore them. Don't engage with them again however much they entreat you to do so. Ensure that they understand this and secure their unqualified commitment if you can.

It may also help to have a few things to counter them with just in case they fail to get the message and act upon it. This should only be considered as a last resort and is best done through a legal representative, depending upon whether the other party's actions escalate into the murky and illegal worlds of harassment or stalking.

Remember, people who add no value to your life have no right to be in it. All these individuals are inimical to your physical, mental and emotional health. They are not worthy to be your 'friend'.

" Life shrinks or expands in proportion to one's courage."

— Anaïs Nin

The following Toxic Termination Process or TTP can work face to face or via email or social networking. An elegantly penned letter can be used if you wish to practice your skills in the fine art of calligraphy. You may like to print the TTP as an aide memoire for what you need to do.

Be assertive, direct and polite and ready to counter any arguments. If all goes to plan, this will be your last interaction with this person, so it's important to get it right. What you are about to do should resonate within their mind and psyche.

And get them out of yours.

Rehearse the scene in your mind and focus on the outcome you want. Consider how they might react, based on your knowledge of their behaviour and psychology.

Will they try to make everything your fault and play on any residual guilt? Will they try to drown you in a lake filled with their own emotional incontinence? Will they resist your logical entreaties vigorously and beg for 'one last chance'? Unfetter your imagination, write down every potential scenario and come up with a range of responses. Use visualisation to practice your reactions and clarify your objectives.

If you have any suspicion that the person might resort to physical violence, exercise extreme caution. You may wish to avoid any physical contact with them. Raise your concerns with a family member, legal representative, law enforcement official or a friend who used to be in the military.

Always stay safe.

Once the person is out of your life, move on and don't pay any mental attention to them. You might find this difficult initially, so have a number of things to do that will enable and facilitate this process.

Your engagement with this person may have formed some neural connections within your brain – remember the expression 'neurons that fire together wire together'. Luckily neuroplasticity (the ability of the brain to create new patterns of thinking) and neurogenesis (the brain, in particular the hippocampus, creating new brain cells) are your friends here.

You are looking to create new, powerful, associative and transformative neural patterns, which, as a fortunate and serendipitous by-product, also serve to terminate any negative associations with a toxic person.

Take this as an opportunity to do different things and give your brain a real workout. Find new friends, challenging and stimulating things to do, practice mindfulness meditation. Read 'The Power of Now' by Eckhart Tolle, a book that will nicely root you in the eternal present, free from the grasping encumbrances of the dead hand of the past and pointless speculation on the unborn future.

You are looking to get rid of any trace of this person that lingers around your mind to ensure any effect on you is eradicated.

Identification

You've been through the Friend Ranking Quadrant (FRQ) and worked out whom you want to keep in your life and, by process of elimination, which you want to permanently extract.

You will have a hit list of at least one Toxic to contend with. If you have several Toxics, run through the exercise again to ensure that your first analysis is correct. If you do have more than one to contend with you have two options.

The first is to perform TTP on all of them, more or less simultaneously; the second is to target them one at a time. Both approaches clearly have their pros and cons. If you can eliminate all of them at the same time you've achieved something quite dramatic and should feel very proud. However, if there is any linkage between the Toxics, they may try to gang up on you.

Picking them off one by one and keeping them isolated is a longer-term process that may require more time, effort and energy. The end result, however, is what you are looking for and this may be a 'no pain, no gain' scenario that you can't avoid.

Life sometimes throws you challenges to toughen you up and sharpen your insight and experience. Some people welcome them – which is not an excuse to invite more Toxics into your life.

SWOT Analysis

This is a classic situational analysis tool used by many business organisations to identify their strengths, weaknesses, opportunities and threats. This can include market position, financing, quality of personnel, effectiveness of management, systems used, competitive analysis and so on.

You can use this as a tool to plan TTP. The SWOT analysis should cover both you and the Toxic, which is why knowledge of their backstory may be useful. Try also to factor in any environmental or contextual issues – where you will perform TTP (physical or remote), other parties involved and so on.

Strengths:

You – motivation and intent (you know the person is toxic and want them out of your life). Technique – you know the process and how and where you will apply it. You have a strong personality, which you have worked on, and have planned every conceivable variation on events.

Toxic – you don't quite know how they will behave and they can be quite tenacious. Even now, it's unclear what behaviours they will utilise. Evidence and analysis leads you to believe that they will move on to vex another party, but you are only eighty five percent sure.

Weaknesses:

You – slight feelings of guilt that some of this may be your doing, and that the Toxic is behaving the way they do because you didn't communicate earlier that you wanted nothing to do with them. Therefore they could argue that you were sending misleading messages and try to work a guilt angle on you, which, due to your upbringing, you know might be effective.

Toxic – they are very over emotional. As an analytical person, this is a trend you detest and usually handle by being cold and indifferent, which they find very difficult to deal with. The more emphatic they get, the colder your response. They already have this pattern formed, so if necessary, you are comfortable with exploiting it.

Opportunities:

You – you know what you want and can set the meeting or email sequence as soon as possible. You know the Toxic dislikes change and surprises, so you can wrong foot them by acting quickly and striking with your carefully honed TTP missive when they are least expecting it.

Toxic – unclear what their options are at this stage, you've factored everything you can think of into the mental dress rehearsal you've performed, and are sufficiently savvy to counter anything that, short of them pulling a gun on you, comes leftfield.

Threats:

You – nobody can predict one hundred percent what will happen in any give situation. You've planned as best as you can and thought it through and can see no downside. Once again, your flexible mindset should serve you well. You'll be meeting in a public place, so the worst you can expect is a series of teary tantrums and childish and noisy displays of disquietude.

Toxic – you have been the centre of the Toxic's obsession for far longer than you wish to remember. You are now absenting yourself permanently from the Toxic's life and this will hit them hard, perhaps harder than you or they know. What the Toxic will do next is unclear, probably to them as much as to you. You have decided that they are bad for you to be around and ultimately your happiness and peace of mind are all that matters to you, so you have no choice but to continue with the strategy you've committed to.

Negotiation (Optional)

This is the very reasonable 'one last chance' stage of TTP. You are telling the Toxic that it's your way or the highway.

Note that this stage is optional. If you know that you definitely want the Toxic out of your life, you should go straight to Final Rites and Burial. If you think there is some remote chance that the Toxic will change their behaviour in a way that is acceptable to you, negotiation is your only realistic option. Make sure that you are choosing this in a clear-headed analytical way, and are not allowing emotion or sentiment to cloud your judgment.

If the negotiation fails and the Toxic, verbally agreeing to everything you say, reverts to their old behaviour as soon as they get the opportunity, you have wasted a lot of time and energy and give the Toxic more power. This could make the rejection stages of TTP more difficult than they need to be. So exercise extreme care if you go this route.

When negotiating, let them know there is a problem and that they are the problem. You don't want to get into long-winded circuitous arguments as to who's at fault. All you are focusing on is that they are bad for you, their behaviour is unacceptable and that, unless the behaviour changes, you do not want them in your life. You can expect a degree of argument and bluster; especially if the Toxic is of the mentation that nothing is ever their fault.

Make it clear, concise and unambivalent to ensure that they understand that this is their very last chance. Furthermore, that you are setting a period of time in which you are expecting them to make the required changes.

Accept that you may need to modify some of your behaviour – negotiation is a matter of give and take and trading concessions. However, make them aware that there are boundaries that they must not cross and that if they do, that's it. They're out of your life forever. Get them to understand the consequences of transgression and commit to change. A written statement or email to this effect is an effective way to seal the deal.

The Toxic, gushing in agreement, may want a hug or some physical reassurance at this stage.

Should you do it? It depends on your reading of the Toxic. They might think that they've got away with something and that you are not serious. So on balance, don't – keep everything professional, cordial and business like. Also make sure they know that you are monitoring their progress, and that any transgression on their part will prove fatal.

Stage One – Final Rites

Step 1.

It's time to cut this individual out of your life forever. They've had multiple chances but won't change. They just can't make the effort to change and will never redeem themselves, so let them go. You've completed your analysis and made the decision. It's time to initiate the Termination Sequence.

Step 2.

The message can be delivered in person, by letter or email. Work out what you are most comfortable doing and what, given your knowledge of the person, will be most effective. Remember, this is non-negotiable, so craft your message thoroughly so that even the densest Toxic will understand and act upon it.

Step 3.

Tell them how the way they treat you makes you feel and that you won't accept this from anyone. (Rehearse this a few times – be strong and assertive.) Show them who the boss is and lay down the rules. Advise them how toxic they are and how you refuse to continue to tolerate them. Your communication should be direct, polite and balanced. Whatever they do, you do not descend into being ignoble or over-emotional, and you therefore retain the moral high ground.

Step 4.

Make them aware that you no longer wish to communicate or spend any time with them. Ensure this message is short, crisp and to the point. Get them to agree to this – you want a commitment from them that they will never contact you again in any way, shape or form.

The majority of people have a sense of honour, if so bring out this fine quality by reminding them of it. They might even feel better for the duration of your conversation. But clearly don't let them use this as an argument to stay in touch.

Step 5.

Cut off their oxygen supply by being succinct. Don't give them any information they might use to hang a counter argument on or interpret in a way to suggest there is any hope for them. Just say no if they ask for something. Don't take anything they offer so you can avoid any potential guilt trips. Ensure you control the interaction and dialogue at all stages.

How should you craft your argument? It needs to be effective and concise. You could see yourself as a barrister finalising their case and presenting it to both judge and jury. If necessary, you need to be very focused, determined and even brutal – whatever it takes to reinforce the message and get rid of them. You don't want to make them into an enemy, though sometimes this is unavoidable.

And, though tempting, you may not want to go as far as the following quote from an awesome TV drama (though if you are dealing with a particularly aggressive and abusive long-term Toxic, you might find parts of it inspirational):

Stage Two – Burial

Step 1.

Now deliver on your promise and cut them out of your life completely – don't answer emails or calls, do nothing to encourage them. Blank them. Just get rid of them.

If the person has any decency, honour or integrity, they will respect your wishes and leave you alone.

Step 2.

Be aware that some people will try every trick in the book to argue against you and insinuate their way back into your life (this is why you need to gain their assent and commitment, outlined in paragraph 4 above). So dress-rehearse your strategy and work out their possible responses. Don't fall for guilt trips, hoovering or anything else they might try in the future.

Step 3.

Feel no guilt or remorse. You are doing what's best for you to make you happy. Toxic individuals are full of poison for your mind and soul, so getting rid of this unnecessary negative force empowers you to live your best life.

To you, this person no longer exists and is effectively dead to you. Resurrection is not an option.

Step 4.

If necessary change your email addresses, sites you often frequent and so on. If you are a social networking aficionado, ensure your security is set at the absolute maximum. Or just do something more interesting in the non-virtual world.

Step 5.

You want to ensure that this individual cannot communicate with you in any way. If you need an existing email address, just set up a rule to move any communication from them into a designated folder so that you don't even read it. You may choose to keep a record of their communications but do you really need to read them?

Step 6.

Be very wary of any online request to be your friend from someone you do not know. Vet everybody. A degree of vigilance will work wonders for your self-interest and reduce the possibility of the Toxic sneaking back into your life.

Step 7.

Obviously you do not follow the toxic individual on any social network, blog or similar site. Your objective is a clean, clear break so you don't do anything to compromise this. Out of sight is out of mind, right?

Step 8.

You may consider retaining copies of any existing correspondence in case you need it for your legal advisor, authorities etc., depending on the legal framework within your jurisdiction.

If you don't want this material polluting your house or PC/Mac/tablet/phone, keep it elsewhere, on a memory stick, with your legal representative or on a secure cloud server. Treat it with caution and quarantine it – like a piece of malware.

Step 9.

If the person proves intractable and attempts to get in contact, consider rerouting any further communication to your legal representative to establish if there are grounds for proceedings to be taken.

Step 10.

You want the toxic individual out of your life permanently - this means physically and psychologically. This entails not thinking about them, not fuelling them or giving them any headspace. You could do a short rite of exorcism if this works for you, spend more time with your real friends, sing a song (ding dong, the Toxic's gone), tell a joke, have a drink, or go for a decent meal at a good restaurant.

Step 11.

Ultimately, live the best life that you can.

Enjoy yourself, be creative, have fun, make new friends, learn how to fly and get your pilot's licence, master a musical instrument to really engage all parts of your brain (keyboards are good), get a different job, travel extensively.

See the departure of the Toxic as a wakeup call to change your life.

Do things that fully engage you in the moment so that you don't feel any compulsion to ruminate over the past. You won't be moping when you're bobsleighing around St. Moritz at 90 mph or leaping rooftop to rooftop in Paris whilst you perfect your parkour skills.

Choose whatever works for you. Moving on and being your best self is the most effective way of disengaging and distancing from malign toxic influences. And you can do the truly spontaneous Duchene smile. You know they'll just hate the fact that you are having a happier, more successful time without them than they could even begin to conceive.

Step 12.

Be vigilant and self-aware so that you do not attract such people in the future. Work on your self-esteem and self-confidence if you find that prolonged exposure to a Toxic has caused you to lose confidence in your ability to read people. Building your self-esteem and self-confidence will help immeasurably when it comes to attracting the right friends and creating healthy relationships.

Be Aware

That ditching your Toxic may cause you to lose other friends especially if the Toxic has managed to make you appear toxic for ditching them. There's little if anything you can do about this. Sometimes freedom comes at a cost.

Perhaps you need a new set of people in your life anyway.

# Chapter 9

## Exercises To Try

While one on one time with a therapist is going to be required in order to make it through the complicated process of recovering from a lifetime of dealing with a narcissistic mother, it is important to understand that change is possible thanks to a concept known as neural plasticity. While you work on dealing with your larger issues in the long-term the following exercises can help you cope with the symptoms of these issues in the short-term.

*Watch for cognitive distortions*: In order to restructure your thoughts, the first thing that you are going to need to do is become aware of when your thoughts are distorting the truth of the matter. These types of distortions can come in a wide variety of shapes and sizes, but the one thing they will have in common is that they will try and force you to see the world differently than it truly is. As such, the way to ensure that this ceases to be an issue is to become more aware of when they are affecting the way you respond to specific situations.

Once you are more aware of when cognitive distortion is occurring, you will then be able to more easily respond to the situation in a way that is productive, instead of simply being along for the ride. To start, you simply need to ask yourself how else you could be thinking about whatever it is that is going on. You may also find it helpful to consider what the worst-case scenario in the current situation could be. With that in mind, you will likely find that you start to feel better when you consider how likely that scenario is to actually occur.

With this done, it is important to act upon the information that you have gained, especially if you have determined that the cognitive distortion is invalid. Going through the process of determining the accuracy of a cognitive distortion is meaningless if you don't follow through on what you have learned. The change doesn't need to be immediate, after all some distortions will likely have been with you for a very long time, however, as long as you acknowledge what you have learned and remain open to new experiences moving forward, you will find that your old cognitive distortions can give way to a new way of seeing the world.

*Cognitive restructuring:* If you looked at another person's cognitive distortions you would likely find them easy to dispute. For example, no matter how much a friend of yours feels as though they are absolutely the worst, you can see why this is untrue. However, when it comes to your personal cognitive distortions, you will likely find them much more difficult to overcome which is why they persist in the first place. You will find that, without help, you will continue to believe in your own cognitive distortions no matter how they actually differ from the way the world really is.

Luckily there are several different ways to tear down your cognitive distortions, no matter how deeply held they might be. These techniques can be used at any time you find yourself coming up against a cognitive distortion and, with enough practice, you will find yourself coming up against them less and less often and they will be replaced with balanced, accurate thoughts instead.

For starters, you are going to want to utilize what is known as Socratic questioning to determine the validity of your thoughts out of the gate. The Greek philosopher Socrates always emphasized the importance of questions as a means of exploring otherwise complicated ideas and uncovering inherent assumptions. To make use of his method when it comes to cognitive distortions, you will want to assess that you are looking at things through their filter by asking a number of different questions of yourself. These questions include:

- Is this a realistic thought?

- What is the basis for the thought, is it feelings or is it facts?

- Does this thought have any evidence to back it up?

- Is it possible that I am misinterpreting the evidence based on cognitive distortion?

- Is this situation more complicated than simply black or white?

- Is this a habitual thought or is it supported by the facts of the current situation?

When you come across a negative thought that you just can't shake, take the time to test it out instead. This is a great way to take whatever it is that you are thinking about and figure out an answer, one way or another. For example, if you are angry because you feel too stressed at work to take breaks, then this is something that can easily be tested. You would simply act normally one week and rate your overall effectiveness, and then take more breaks the next week, rate your overall effectiveness and then compare the two. This takes the entire process out of the theoretical and puts it fully in the realm of something that can be tested with results that can be taken to the bank.

If the thought process that you are stuck on can't be easily tested, then you may instead find it useful to look at all the available evidence and see where that gets you. To do so, all you need to do is to take a long hard look at the situation in question and then write down everything that supports whatever your thought process says is going on and then everything that supports the idea that your perception of the situation is warped. When you are staring at the evidence in the face you will find that it is much harder to hide from the truth than when everything is simply floating around in your head instead.

*Break common patterns:* Finally, knowing what you now know, the only thing left to do is to break out of the patterns that have formed around the cognitive distortions you are trying to break free from. This is going to be much easier said than done, however, especially if the habits are extremely deeply ingrained. As such, you may want to start by changing small aspects of the negative habits first, before working up to a full-blown change. This will give your ingrained neural pathways some time to start expanding before jumping to something entirely new and different.

Remember, it takes about 30 days to build a new habit from scratch, which means that once you have reached the point where you are ready to give the old habit the boot for good, you should be ready to immediately start something new to take its place. Having a new habit to replace the old one with directly will give your mind something new to latch onto, giving it a place to put its focus while you focus on the more serious task of kicking the old habit to the curb. Keep in mind that forming a new habit is a chance to improve some aspect of your everyday life, choose wisely and keep it up once you start. While the going may be tough in the interim, in just one month you will be settled into your new routine and it will have all been worth it.

*Positive self-talk*: If you have ever heard a little voice in your mind telling you that you aren't good enough, smart enough, strong enough or fast enough to complete a given task then you have experienced negative self-talk. While most people hear this voice occasionally, and more or less ignore it, for those with lingering issues related to a narcissistic mother, this type of negative self-talk often never stops. While most people will be able to ignore it for a time, eventually it starts to work as a mantra and seep into the very fabric of your thought processes.

That is to say that this level of repetition can have a far greater impact than you may initially realize as eventually, you may come to believe it is true regardless of what the true state of the world might be. If you aren't careful, what starts out as simple heckling could ultimately redefine the very way you see yourself, how you think about yourself and how you define yourself with thoughts and actions.

In order to combat this insidious tendency, your best defense is its opposite or positive self-talk. Positive self-talk is an exercise you can do whenever you feel the need or whenever you are having a particularly negative thought about yourself. Getting started is exceedingly simple, all you need to do is mentally deny the negative thought and replace it with a positive one instead. The denial is an important step in the process as it is important that you get in the habit of actively denying the negative self-talk for the best results.

The first step towards fixing the problem is being aware of it, if you have already practiced meditation than the concept of seeing thoughts without interacting with them will already be familiar to you. Basically, what you want to do is take the time to become fully aware of every thought that passes through your mind. Common forms of negative self-talk involve the phrases "I can't" or "I have never been able to", these are common answers to fixed mindset patterns and should be avoided at all costs. If you find that you mind to be full of these sorts of statements, respond to them by asking "why can't I" and see where this train of thought leads you.

It can be easy to let thoughts exist in the background while another task is front and center but for this exercise, it is important to focus on those other thoughts for long enough to ensure that they aren't harboring thoughts which might promote a fixed mindset. The trick is hearing these thoughts without interacting with them, the goal is to find them and let them go without giving them any extra mental real estate. While you are working on not interacting with these disruptive thoughts it can be helpful to instead think, "Abort, abort" after any negative self-talk has been perceived. This command will break up whatever thought process you were currently working through and allow you to eject the negative thought more easily.

If you find yourself having difficulty with this particular tip, another option is to wear a rubber band or hair tie around your wrist so that every time you catch yourself in negative self-talk you can snap your wrist. This will serve two functions. The first is it will draw your attention to the negative self-talk so that you become aware of it and can then deal with it accordingly. The second is to distract your mind from the negativity long enough that the negative thought does not have time to propagate.

*Mindfulness meditation:* Meditation can work wonders. Mindfulness activities including meditation can bring about a high volume of the hippocampus and amygdala and reduce stress. One research project showed evidence that just 27 minutes a day of meditation or other mindfulness techniques can accomplish improvements in hippocampus and amygdala performance and relieve stress.

While the ultimate goal of mindfulness meditation is to quiet the mind in an effort to find a state of internal calm despite the hustle and bustle of the outside world, many people find it difficult to achieve this state right out of the gate. Instead, you will likely find it easier to start to supplant any thoughts you might have by focusing all of your attention on the signals that your senses are relaying to you to the exclusion of everything else. While you might not feel as though you are receiving much data on the physical world, especially if you are practicing in a quiet, temperate space, the truth of the matter is that your brain naturally filters out approximately eighty percent of everything it receives, you just need to get in the habit of tapping into it.

With practice, you will learn to tune out your more common thoughts and to instead tune into what is going on around you. When you do this, it is important to simply take in the information your senses are providing without thinking about it too deeply or passing judgement on what you perceive. Judging tends to lead to additional thoughts or, even worse, comparison of the present group of situations to those of the past which is more likely to pull you out of the moment and make finding the state of calm you are looking for even more difficult than it is likely to be, especially when you are just getting started.

Remember, the goal with mindfulness meditation is to get as close to existing at the moment as possible and ignoring everything outside of your current surroundings as much as possible. To reach the required state you are going to want to start by focusing on your breathing, the feel of the air slowly entering and exiting your lungs as well as any smells or tastes that go along with this practice. From there you can then expand the sphere of observation to any other sensations that your body might be experiencing, all the while going deeper into yourself in search of the point where your mind ceases to form new thoughts and simply exists in a state of peaceful relaxation.

Mindfulness is not necessarily quieting the mind or finding an eternal state of calmness. The goal here is simple. We want to pay attention to the moment we are in without judging. When we judge a thought or something we may have done in the past, we tend to dwell on it. That isn't living in the moment and is not conducive to mindful meditation. While this is easier said than done, it is a crucial step to mindful meditation. With practice, it will be easy to achieve. Be mindful of the moment, of your senses and your surroundings.

Take notice of the times you are passing judgment while practicing. Make a note of them and move on. It is easy for our minds to get lost in thought. Mindfulness meditation is the art of bringing yourself back to the moment, over and over, as many times as it takes. Don't get discouraged. In the beginning, you will find your mind wanders a lot. Reel it back in and keep moving forward. Even if your mind does happen to wander—and it will—don't be hard on yourself. Acknowledge whatever thoughts pop up, put them to the side and get back on track.

*Keep it up*: This list is by no means exhaustive, and sometimes a setback can really upset your plans to solve some very real problems in your life. Think of the destruction, the lost friendships, and maybe the lost opportunities. Opportunities to make more of yourself or the opportunities to get to know people throughout your life somewhat better.

Remember not to get discouraged. Remember that you do not need to be perfect all the time and don't ignore your feelings too much. Cut yourself some slack. Do not be so hard on yourself. You want to form new habits, new coping skills.

There's no way to find out more about yourself if you do not put in the hard work. Try to sweat it out and try some of the ideas here that require you to leave a seated position. A runner may stumble in the field sometimes, but he gets up and continues to run until he reaches the finish line. The true winner is not who reached the finish line first, but those that didn't give up. At times you may still have difficulty managing your emotions and holding back your anger, but that's normal and understandable. We're not perfect and may go the different way sometimes. But always remember what your goal is and how much improvement you've made so far.

# Chapter 10

## Public And Private Images Of Narcissists

Narcissists are good actors. This is one of their manipulative skills. They need histrionic skills to gaslight their victims and assert their dominance. The better you understand their good acting skills, the better you'll be able to deal with them.

Narcissists can be charming when they want to. I mean, they are great charmers! They have the uncanny ability to sweep you off your feet on a first encounter. You'll love them! They are astute in reading their scripts and in interpreting their roles perfectly well. That's why they are good actors!

And what's their scripts? You and me. Their scripts are people they meet and situations they find themselves. They will enchant you if they need something from you. They may like something or dislike it, depending on the script. For example, a narcissist may actually dislike your taste of music, but can tell you she loves in order to get into you.

A narcissist can pretend to like your favorite celebrity if that will help her cause. I have to warn you, narcissists are good actors—better than Angelina Jolie and Dwayne Johnson combined. Okay, that may be an exaggeration. But you get my point? Good, that's all that matters.

You really have to understand this aspect of narcissists, because this is one aspect people don't really know about them. And this is why people, even some relatives and friends, don't know the ordeal a child is going through at home. The reason is because the narcissist is playing the role of the best mom outside and villain at home.

So I'll be devoting this chapter to reveal their various images and roles. I could write a whole book on this alone. To help you have a concrete understanding of the acting skills of narcissists, I'll be using tangible imageries to explain.

## The human chameleon

Narcissists change attributes more than chameleons. That comparison may be hyperbolic, but it's not that off, if you've met a narcissist. Chameleons change color for various reasons: to adapt to their environments: to adjust their body temperature to that of their environment, to trap unsuspecting preys and to protect themselves from predators.

Does this sound familiar? Narcissist acts in order to:

## Adapt to their environments

Like chameleons, narcissist need to properly adapt to their environments before they begin their operation. This is the first thing they do. Don't let their self-absorption and insensitivity fool you into thinking they don't know what's going on around them. They do!

They do more than you realize, and this is one of their advantage. It takes dark wisdom to foster division between people. It takes some ingenuity to gaslight and exploit others for selfish purposes. So wake up from your slumber! Narcissists are much more alert to their environment.

They are great readers of situations and good calculators. They may appear slow like chameleons, but their shrewdness makes up for their seeming tardiness. To adapt to their environment, narcissist do a lot of scripts reading.

## Adjust their body temperature to that of their environment

While chameleons adjust their body temperature to match that of their environment, narcissists adjust their mood and character to match that of those around them who they stand to benefit from. Narcissists will never adjust their mood for those they can bully.

This ability endears narcissists to outsiders. A woman can be a narcissist in her home and no one in her church may know anything about it. They are that good! Your narcissistic mom may put up her best behavior in public, to the admiration of everyone—including you. You may find yourself wondering if this is actually your mom. She has mastered the art of playing the mood.

## Trap unsuspecting preys

Have you seen the chameleon's tongue before? It's a long thingy that's super-fast. The chameleon uses it to draw in unsuspecting preys into the vaults of its stomach. Narcissists are like this too. They may not be fast as chameleons, but like their reptile counterparts, their attack is sudden and fast.

They first start by disguising as good people. They will make every effort to make their victims feel comfortable before they strike. It's like the proverbial folklore in which the animal kingdom decided to kill the proud elephant. The only way to do this was to make the elephant the king.

Amidst pomp and pageantry, they led the elephant to the throne that was placed on a very deep hole. Thud! The big guy crashed into the hole trumpeting as he went down. That was the end of that elephant. Moral of the story: The narcissist doesn't mind making you a king if that's how he'll get rid of you.

## Protect themselves from predators.

Though narcissists live in imaginary world, they understand the dangers of real life. This is to be expected since the trauma of real life was what encouraged their narcissism in the first place. If pretending to be who they are not will protect their dominance and selfish interests, they will do it.

They can even obey or submit themselves for the time being to protect themselves. But be assured that they will strike at the opportune moment, and they will strike hard.

Having multiple images is very essential for the survival of narcissists. It's their way of being in control. They require a public image and a private image to be on top of their game. The public image is a nice, easygoing, and lovely one. This isn't their true nature. It's a false projection of their true self. The private image, on the other hand, is who they truly are. Your true character is the quality you exhibit when you're alone. It's pure and unpretentious.

Typical Images of Narcissists

Narcissists can be compared to many things. Narcissists are:

## Like the earth

Narcissists are like the earth. How? Glad you asked. The earth is dark on one side and bright on the other side. This explains night and day. When the United States is sunny, the United Kingdom will be moony. As the earth spins around its own axis, one side faces the sun and the other side backs the sun. The side that faces the sun is the day and the other side is the night.

Narcissists spins around their own axis too! They show good side to some and bad side to others, depending on their mood, relationship, and selfish interest. Their public image is sunny, lovely and beautiful to behold. You'd love it. But their private image is often dark and freezing cold. This is their true nature.

Their dark side is insensitive, emotionless, abusive, divisive, domineering, cocky, and every other trait I've addressed earlier about NDP. This is the side that's hidden, but it's the side that's venomous.

## Demons at home

On their good day, narcissists can be very cruel, but on their bad day they can be monstrous. This image is of course shown to those close to them. It's their private image. They are venomous monsters that victimize their victims. They are unstoppable in their quest to assert their dominance.

They are merciless and vicious. They will do almost anything to achieve their objectives. They will gaslight, victimize, traumatize, and even pauperize to have their way. Show me a more formidable monster!

## Angels outside

Narcissists are angels outside. They are likable and social. They are good actors, remember? Outsiders see them as those who can't even hurt a fly. They are congenial and fun to be with. This unreal side of them is part of their divisive strategy. They need to put on a show so that outsiders won't suspect a thing.

Chapter Summary

Image is everything to narcissists. They need this talent for survival and dominance. Please, never underestimate the acting skills of narcissists. If your mom is a narcissist, or you know a narcissist, you've already seen it in action.

Narcissists must have two images: a public image and a private image. The images you see are the ones they want you to see. They are like chameleons, so they can neatly hide their flaws. They can pretend to be who they aren't perfectly, because their whole life is imaginary. You must be very careful when you're dealing with them.

# Chapter 11

## A Narcissistic Mother's Daughter

Symptoms in a narcissistic mother-daughter relationship are not exclusive to the mother. Daughters who have been raised by narcissistic mothers are also subjected to experiencing many of their painful symptoms that can lead to many problems in the future. You need to take the time to look at yourself as a part of the equation to see what symptoms you are experiencing, and to understand how they may be influencing you to experience more problems or abuse in your adult life.

Looking at your symptoms can be painful because you are going to have to face everything that you now experience and understand that this was all due to your mother. You might feel an intense amount of rage, sadness, pain, grief, guilt, or other emotions relating to these discoveries, so I strongly encourage you to make sure you can speak to someone you trust after reading this chapter. Being prepared to receive support as soon as you need it when difficult emotions or memories come up can be helpful in your recovery from this abuse.

## You May Be Chronically Ashamed of Yourself

Daughters of narcissistic mothers are known for experiencing chronic shame in their lives, particularly around everything relating to who they are and what they do. It may feel like there is no limit to the shame that you experience, and that you tend to experience it in many different ways.

The shame that you experience now stems from always being made to feel inadequate as a child. Narcissistic mothers tend to be especially threatened by their daughters, which means that the level of abuse that you have experienced in terms of being put down and bullied is likely enormous. There is a good chance that your entire childhood was spent with you being told the many reasons as to why you were a bad person, and why you were not good enough. You were probably told that you were not deserving, not pretty, not smart, not worthy, and many other untrue things that were said to get you to stop bringing attention to yourself.

By making you feel horrible about yourself, your mother could feel confident that you would stay quiet and hidden all on your own so that she did not have to attempt to do it for you. She also would not have to take responsibility for dragging your name through the mud or spreading bad rumors about you, which is a common narcissistic behavior known as "smearing." In some ways, your mom may have even used your low self-esteem to increase her sense of importance, such as by bragging about how she had to stand up for you or try to build you up in certain situations because you lack self-esteem. Of course, she would never mention that your lack of self-esteem came from her in the first place because this would take away from her perfect image.

As an adult, you may now experience chronic shame around everything in your life even when you know it is not needed. You might hold yourself to unreasonably high standards, feel guilty about things that are normal human experiences, and attempt to behave like a superhuman because you have been told that you are not good enough. These behaviors are likely both an effort to be seen as a good person and an effort to avoid being abused any further because in your childhood you would be abused if you did not fight to achieve these unreasonable standards. This shame is extremely toxic, painful, and life-altering, which is why we are going to spend so much time addressing and healing it in part 2 of this book.

## Childhood Abuse May Lead to Adulthood Abuse or Toxic Relationship Patterns

Any form of childhood abuse can lead to children growing up and entering abusive and toxic relationships, and a child abused by a narcissist is no different. It is possible that as an adult you are now finding yourself in many toxic relationships, or relationships that are even downright abusive. You might feel like you have some sort of hidden "signal" that somehow calls in people who will take advantage of you, bully you, or abuse you through narcissism in your adult life. Many daughters of narcissistic mothers feel as though they cannot get away from narcissism, even though they were sure that leaving their childhood homes would suffice.

The reason why you may be experiencing toxic or abusive relationships now in adulthood is that you have never been taught boundaries or important self-care steps in life. Being raised by someone who commanded you to live your entire life based on her needs and desires has resulted in you not knowing how to fully stand up for yourself and take care of yourself in relationships now. This may be painful to admit, but, indeed, it is likely the reason why this is happening. If you notice that you seem to be surrounded by people who abuse you or take advantage of you and you cannot seem to understand why this happens, there is a good chance that it is a product of your groomed behaviors.

## You May Reflect Some of Your Mother's Symptoms

As a daughter of a narcissist, this can be one of the more scary symptoms that you may face. It is one thing to feel unsafe with others, but to feel unsafe within yourself and to recognize yourself behaving in ways that you do not like can be downright terrifying. There is a chance that now as an adult you reflect some of your mother's symptoms, and this can lead to an intense fear that you are going to become abusive toward someone you love just like she did. You may not understand why these behaviors or exist or have any clarity around how far they will develop too, leaving you feeling powerless and as though it may be inevitable for you to follow in her damaging footsteps.

Believe it or not, even though many people do not like to talk about this point, it is quite common in those who survive narcissistic abuse from a parent specifically. The reason for this symptom is that as a child you are supposed to be raised by a nurturing guardian who can guide you to learn how to navigate various parts of life. Ideally, a healthy guardian should have taught you how to deal with difficult emotions, conflict, expectations, self-esteem, insecurities, and other natural parts of life. Unfortunately, you were raised by a mom who did not know how and who regularly modeled extremely poor examples of how an individual should deal with these things. As an adult, you reflecting this behavior is unlikely to be you displaying true narcissism and more likely to be you displaying poor coping methods in life. With proper healing and efforts, you should be able to identify new ways for you to cope with things in life, enabling you to move beyond the patterns of repeating your mothers' behavior due to not knowing a better way.

## There May Be the Feeling of a Deep Void in Your Life

One of the most painful things that I have experienced as a daughter of a narcissist, even to this day, is that void that you feel in yourself and your life around your mother. As an adult, you may now find yourself longing for a positive relationship with your mother, possibly to the point where you keep attempting to have a better relationship with her only to find yourself trapped in the cycle again and again. This is a common experience for daughters of narcissistic mothers and I want to tell you right now that this is not a poor reflection of you, instead, it is a painful reflection of your reality.

Even when you heal yourself from your mother's abuse, you are likely to find yourself in moments where you wish you had a healthy, supportive mother to rely on. You might even recall the times your mother showed you her charming mask, leading you to feel like maybe you can call her for support on just this one thing, hoping that she will offer that type of charm and support once again. It can be painful when you realize that your mother is unavailable to offer you the support and the love that you need, and even more painful when you realize that she has no idea why you feel so disconnected and alone in the world due to her treatment. This is a natural part of the recovery and healing process, and in time it does become a lot easier to navigate. While the pain itself is always there, you will find that you become much stronger in healing that pain and coping with it when it rears its head. This way, you do not put yourself in a game of yo-yo with trying to get your mother to be the woman you need her to be when she truly can't be.

# Chapter 12

## Beating The Narcissists At Their Own Game

Now, we're going to look at the various techniques you can use to foil the narcissist at every turn. I did promise I would give you these tools. If you'd like to learn how to drive the narcissist nuts and beat them at their very own game, then let's proceed.

Be Unpredictable

The narcissist expects you to behave in certain ways every time they do something manipulative or hurtful to you. More often than not, when the narcissist provokes you, you have set ways of responding. You've both done this song and dance long enough that you don't even realize that you have the option of reacting differently.

The one thing the narcissist is never quite prepared for when they attempt to hurt or provoke you is indifference. They also don't expect you to be happy, or joyful. They don't expect you to be stubborn about what you want, or to act from a place of security when they torment you.

What you want to do when the narcissist is tormenting you is the exact opposite of whatever you'd like to do in that moment.

For instance, rather than cry, or lash out angrily, you can choose to smile or laugh instead. It helps you feel a lot better, and will get rid of all feelings of anxiety and stress. Let's make this as practical as possible.

Say, at the moment, the narcissist is triangulating you. One thing you can do is simply keep your facial expression neutral, while you switch to a different topic. Another thing you could do is simply choose not to engage in the conversation to begin with. If the narcissist is triangulating you with a stranger in your presence (one the narcissist has no sexual or romantic ties with, to be precise) then you could be extra friendly and warm towards the stranger the narcissist is trying to triangulate you with. Or, you could simply leave the room. Choosing to take the high road by leaving will definitely not go unnoticed by the stranger. One way to tell for sure that the narcissist is triangulating you is to focus your attention on someone else besides the person the narcissist is actively engaging with in your presence. If the narc is triangulating, her attention will turn from her conversation to yours.

If the narc is stonewalling you, then it's certain they expect you to try to claw through their defenses to get to them. Rather than anxiously struggle to get back in their good graces, choose that time to do something for yourself. Do something you enjoy. Go tend to the garden, or pick up a book, hit the gym or take a walk, call a lovely friend, or see the nice neighbors. Keep your phone off while you do whatever is the opposite of what they expect from you. If you used to beg for mercy in the past, just stop. It's a great chance for you to get some practice going No Contact. So, do that instead.

Is the narc trying the hoover maneuver in the hopes of sucking you back in? Doubtless, he expects you to fall for the empty apologies and the crocodile tears. He thinks your No Contact thing is for show, and nothing more. You'll be back to him in no time. Well, this time, choose a different course of action. Block him on all your social media. Ignore him. Act like he does not exist. The more the narcissist attempts to hoover you, the more obvious it becomes that she has lost her hold over you.

Become A Mirror

Let Narcissus see himself in you. What do I mean, exactly? You want to mirror the narcissist. When it comes to dating, pretty solid advice is to mirror your love interest. This way, you won't wind up becoming a little too invested in someone who doesn't care all that much for growing a relationship with you. You can employ this same tactic with the narcissist.

When it comes to mirroring the narcissist, you do not want to reflect his false, charming self to him. What you should mirror instead is his cold, cruel side. When you mirror the narc, what happens is you reduce the level of investment you have in the relationship, and at the same time, you prevent the likelihood of fresh trauma. This will give you the room you need to gather your strength and leave when you're ready. So, when the narcissist grows cold, give her the same treatment. When she withdraws, do the same thing.

Using the Silent Treatment

If you're in a relationship with a narcissist and are preparing yourself psychologically to leave, if the narcissist has just recently abused you or is giving you the silent treatment, it would behoove you to take advantage of that. Encourage the silent treatment to go on. Mirror the narcissist. The time you spend not talking to each other can be invested in taking care of yourself, and nurturing your connection with others. This is a great step to take on your way to full No Contact, by the way.

Put Yourself First

This is the ultimate revenge. The narcissist is used to being the big kahuna, the top dog, el jefe, numero uno. Well, for a change, put yourself first. What this will mean is you've got to be willing to say *NO* to the narc, and you've got to yes yourself back to feeling worthy of the good life has to offer. Do this so you can heal. Do this for yourself. Do this to pay back the narc for all the times they put you in second place, if you ever were on their list of priorities to begin with. From now on, when it comes to you and the narc, you come first.

Step Into The Future

It's good to be mindful and present. However, you need to consider the future. As a victim of narcissistic abuse, the tendency is to keep flipping from the present to the past and back, constantly replaying past trauma, and focusing on how bleak the present moment is. Rather than do that, focus on your future. Ask yourself, if things are this bad now, how much worse will they get? Because, bet your bottom dollar that abuse gets worse over time, not better. Ask yourself what the impact will be on your body, and soul. Ask yourself what dreams you may never accomplish if you don't get out while you can.

Ask yourself if you really want to bring kids into the world with this person as a co-parent. If you've already got kids, ask yourself what your abusive, toxic relationship is going to your kids' psyches. Ask yourself if you'd be willing to put up with the narc's behavior when they are old and ugly. The fact is that part of their charm is in their attractiveness right now. Would you still look at them in their twilight years and find them beautiful or handsome with that shitty behavior? It's not shallow if you answered no.

If it's a narcissist you're putting up with at work, ask yourself whether it's worth the risk to your career. If it's a friend, ask yourself if it's worth it to stay friends with them when all they ever do is drain you.

Cut Down On Social Media

It almost seems that social media was made for narcissists. They just love to use social media to find ways to make you feel terrible. They make themselves seem like something other than what they truly are, and they enjoy the fact that you can actually see them in action as they triangulate you with others. When you withdraw from the narcissist, it would serve you to keep clear of all social media. Do not give in to the temptation to stalk the narc. You can temporarily disable your accounts on all social media, so you don't fall for all the manipulation. It might not be easy in the beginning, but over time, you'll find you're craving to be in the loop will die down, and you'll feel more relaxed and at ease, which will facilitate your healing from the trauma bonds the narcissist has created between you two.

*Meditate*

Meditation is a great way for you to come to terms with everything that has happened to you so far, as well as to reconnect with who you really are. Chances are you've forgotten who your true self is, on account of all the abuse you've suffered at the hands of the narcissist. However, when you meditate, you begin to find the lost pieces of yourself, so you can put yourself back together again. It's a great aid on the path to recovery and rediscovery of your authentic self. It will also help you become more and more detached from the narcissist, reducing any impulse to return to your vomit.

No More Rewards for Terrible Behavior

The narcissist is an adult toddler, plain and simple. If you keep giving them sweets every time they do something terrible, what do you expect them to do? Of course, they're going to keep acting terribly! In this situation, after the narcissist has discarded you, when they come back to hoover you and you let them have their way, you have given them some candy again. The best thing for you to do should be to completely ignore them. Stay silent. Don't give them even the start of a word. When you remain completely nonreactive to whatever they say or do, this will drive them nuts. Don't just do it to drive the narcissist nuts, though. Think of it this way: When you were in the narc's life, she never respected you. She never valued you being there. So why bother going back?

Rather than allow the narcissist to idealize you, you idealize yourself for a change. Love bomb yourself. You want to please someone? Please your own self. Why feed the narcissist's illogical, nonexistent fantasies? Channel that energy into your own realistic, attainable dreams. Stop giving your energy, time, and emotion to the narc. No more treats!

Is the narc shedding fake tears again to get you to stay? Come on. You've seen this show before. It happens after every abusive incident. It's at worst, boring and, at best, pathetic and hilarious. You can see through the act now. Pack up and leave. Is the narc going on and on about some prized thing he just acquired or purchased? Look as dull and uninterested as you can. A blank stare ought to do the trick.

Validate Yourself

Stop seeking validation from the narc. It's nice to have validation, true, but you must learn to give it to yourself. This way, you're not giving your power away to others. You don't need to please people to receive validation. You can deliberately choose to congratulate yourself. Become more sensitive to all the wonderful blessings in your life. Become thankful for all your achievements, past and present, great and small. Keep the focus on you, and learn to be comfortable with that.

Get It On The Record

Always save the horrific messages that the narc will inevitably send you. You might need them later. If the narc is out for blood, trying to bring you down with a smear campaign, as a last resort, you could release those messages. However, it doesn't have to come to that. You could simply screenshot the messages and save them to remind you why you never want to have anything to do with this person again, on the off chance that you start to think they really have changed. Document everything: videos, voice notes, chats, emails, and texts. Whenever you're tempted to go back to that horrible drug that is the narc, pull these up and go through them. You'll remember why you don't want to be with them or around them anymore.

### Write It All Down

Get yourself a journal. In this journal, you'll make a list of all the terrible qualities the narcissist in your life has, as well as the experiences you've had with them where they were gaslighting you, or manipulating you in other ways. Keep this journal somewhere the narc won't see it. Keep notes of everything, including the discrepancies between their version of events and yours. Make sure it's all dated. Note your feelings, and note the episodes of abuse. This journal will help you see you're not the crazy one whenever the narc begins with the crazymaking.

### In Summary

As the narcissist idealized you, you must idealize yourself. The difference is because you are capable of empathy, you will come from a place of true love for yourself. Do not waste even a smidge of energy pining over the narc. Idealize yourself, and you'll find that what you've been looking to get from the narc, you could have given yourself all along.

As the narcissist devalues you, you must also devalue what he tries to make you believe about yourself. Understand that the narc sees you as an extension of himself, and as such, the image he's force-feeding you about who you are, is really who he is. So, devalue all that by ignoring it, laughing at it, and seeing it for what it is: futile attempts at manipulation by a pathetic, powerless person.

As the narc discarded you, you must also discard her. Let her go. She is not worthy of you. That's the whole reason she keeps cutting you down. She knows she is not worthy, and she knows she could never measure up to you. So, she hopes to deceive you into forgetting who you really are. Don't fall for it. Discard her.

Now, should you attempt to hoover a narc? The answer to that is no. Hoover yourself. Get to know you again, so you can be reminded of all the many ways you are an awesome badass. It's about time you started treating yourself like the beautiful soul you are.

# Chapter 13

## Statistics On Narcissistic Personality Disorder

Narcissistic personality disorder is prevailing in the ever-growing population of the world, especially in the population of United States. Narcissistic personality disorder can be diagnosed by certain therapies, rehabilitation sessions and treatments, but the problem is that a lot of people, teenagers and specially the parents fail to consult a psychological professional.

A lot of cases have been reported regarding the narcissistic personality disorder and a lot of people are consulting the psychological professionals to get out of this disorder. Narcissistic personality disorder is not inherited or an in-born disorder. Instead, the people develop it over time due to the inferiority complex or due to the societal pressure. The people with narcissistic personality disorder, especially the parents of the children as they have to nurture and raise the children according to the cultural norms.

Narcissistic personality disorder was the subject of many researchers in their studies. So far, they have gathered little data based upon the various cases of narcissistic personality disorder and the types of faces of the maternal or paternal narcissism. Here is the statistical data or findings of the carried out results.

## United States Statistics On Narcissistic Personality Disorder

According to the data gathered, approximately 0.5% of the general population of the United States is suffering from narcissistic personality disorder. Moreover, 2-16% of the population who is seeking help from the medical professionals is reported to have a narcissistic personality disorder.

Almost 6% of the forensic population is suffering from narcissistic personality disorder. But, most of the narcissistic traits present in the general population and in the forensic population are not referred as actual narcissistic personality disorder. Actual narcissistic traits are found in the veterans or the people in military. Almost 20% of the military population is suffering from the narcissistic personality disorder. All six types of narcissistic issues have been reported to the psychological professionals by the military population.

In United States of America, more than 17% of the population of the medical students (first year) is suffering from narcissistic personality disorder. The founder of the IRHRPPE (Institute of Relational Harm Reduction and Public Pathology Education), Sandra L. Brown describes in her online journal at almost 60 million people living in the United States are suffering from the narcissistic traits of the people or the family members around them.

She further says that there are at least 304 million people who are suffering from narcissistic personality disorder in the United States. However, this narcissistic personality disorder population also includes the people with psychological issues and anti-social personality issues. She gives an estimate that at least 12.6 million people are suffering from narcissistic personality disorder with no conscience. It means that the 12.6 million people have no moral values to judge themselves. They comply with what they are feeling, without thinking about the right and wrong.

More than 60.8 million people are adversely affected in the United States by the narcissistic behavior of the narcissistic parent, narcissistic spouse, narcissistic friend or any other narcissistic family member. Furthermore, she makes a clear statement that the 60.8 million people is just a rough estimate as it does not include the children who are secretively being affected by the narcissistic behavior of their parents. Maternal and paternal narcissism is very common in United States.

According to the DSM-5, prevalence of the narcissistic personality disorder in the population of United States is 6% while the prevalence of the anti-social symptoms in the personality is as high as 3.3%.

According to this data, there are more than 326 million in the United States (the population is ever-increasing) and the 6% of the total United States population is suffering from narcissistic personality disorder. This means that approximately, 19,560,000 people are suffering from the narcissistic personality disorder. So, if we combine the population is suffering from the narcissistic personality disorder and the population suffering from anti-social personality disorder. Approximately 697,500,000 people lack empathy or have no conscience. As estimated by Brown, these people affect almost 80.8 million people.

Moreover, the DSM-5 proceeds to inform us that almost 50-75% of all the narcissistic patients are men. The remaining narcissistic patients are women and teenage kids.

## International Statistics on Narcissistic Personality Disorder

Globally, the DSM-5 states that almost 6.2% of the total world population suffers from the narcissistic personality disorder. Narcissistic personality disorder is recognized outside the United States just like in United States. However, the ICD-10 lists 8 faces of narcissistic personality disorder globally.

Narcissistic personality disorder should not be considered lightly as a high unknown percentile of children and adults from around the globe are suffering from the bad effects of maternal narcissism and paternal narcissism. However, despite having narcissistic issues, many parents and fathers are seeking help from the professional psychologists so that they can raise their children in a safe, protective and a healthy environment.

## Maternal narcissism symptoms

Narcissism is a common human practice of feeling important, needing admiration, attention from others, desiring success and love. To an extent, this is quite normal and in most of the situation, it is being considered as an important personality trait which every person must possess but only until it is occasional and mild. It is because it is perfectly fine to be Narcissist to the extent which could not be classed as a disorder.

However, on the other hand, if there is a person who is characterized by Narcissism quite strongly, or the Narcissist personality traits have gone to an extreme in someone, then this is a personality disorder and it will become highly important to pay attention to its treatment. It is because in such situations Narcissism will have the ability to cause functional impairment and distress and even the situation can last for a longer period of time with ease.

If a person possesses a pattern of abnormal behavior for a longer period of time which are particularly characterized by the feeling of self-importance, lack of empathy and excess need for self-admiration. His constant behavior of seeking excess attention and constant admiration can frustrate other people who are in a relationship with the sufferer of this disorder.

Well, to get a better idea about Narcissistic personality disorder it is important to have a look at its basics to get a better idea about the things. Knowing this will surely help you to understand more facts in an effective way with ease.

## Narcissistic personality disorder

A narcissistic personality disorder is one of many other personality disorders. It is a mental sense of suffering from an exaggerated sense self-admiration, self-importance, deep urge of extreme attention, etc. Such people who are suffering from this may have trouble with their relationship because they also have a lack of sympathy and compassion for others.

Such people always feel that they are superior or better than the others who are around them and therefore, they should be treated in special manners accordingly. Well, the fact which remains behind this extreme situation are, this excess confidence is just a mask. Actually, these people have flimsy self-esteem which is vulnerable to even the slightest criticism.

Narcissistic personality disorder can be best defined as a paradox. It is because such people who are suffering from this may act confident and superior but they are lacking at self-esteem and are not actually confident about themselves. They are just craving to seek attention from others and want everyone to praise them only.

Due to their superior attitude, most of the Narcissistic personality disorder sufferers are unable to build positive relationships with others. The Narcissistic personality disorder can become a cause of great disaster not only for the person who is suffering from this but also for the people who are living around that person. These affected persons more often spend much time thinking about themselves only. They often think about the ways to achieve power and success or about the ways to improve their appearance. They try to take advantage of the people who are around them most of the time. The abnormal behavior in most of the people normally begins early in their adulthood or occurs across a different variety of social situations such as in relationships or work life.

Most commonly people who are suffering from this problem are being characterized as self-centered, arrogant, demanding and manipulative. Most of them may also have some sort of splendid illusions or fantasies or could be convinced that they need to have special treatments. In some cases, these people also try to associate themselves with the people they think are unique or have some special capabilities.

It means such people want to be linked with the ones who have been gifted in some way and this is also only for the enhancement of their own self-esteem not to praise the next person. Such people tend to seek excessive attention and admiration and have difficulty when it comes to bear any kind of criticism or defeat.

## Fast facts:

Here are some facts about Narcissism which you must know:

•   Narcissism is a term which has been come from a particular character named as Narcissus in Greek Mythology.

•   Narcissism is being characterized by an extreme sense of self- admiration and self-worth. Features of being prone to irritation, quick to anger and vulnerable to criticism are also associated with this situation.

•   For its diagnosis, symptoms or signs of Narcissism must be chronic and persistent.

## Causes of Narcissism

Well, the exact cause behind the Narcissism is yet unknown because there are different theories about the cause behind Narcissism. Some people think it is a mix of the things which can be ranged from how a person has been raised or how he or she handled different stressing situations.

However, most of the experts tend to apply a biopsychosocial model for this which means that a combination of social, neurobiological, genetic and environmental factors may have played their roles in formulating a Narcissistic personality.

There is also some evidence that this personality disorder can be heritable individuals are likely to develop Narcissism disorder if they have any family history of this disorder. However, in some cases, a specific gene interaction can also contribute to the development of Narcissism personality disorder.

While on the other hand, social and environmental factors are also having a prominent influence on the development of Narcissism disorder. In some cases, Narcissism could develop a weakened attachment with their parents or primary caregivers. This can cause a sense of unconnected and unimportant to others in a child. In some cases, the child may tend to believe that he has some defects in his personality which are making him devalued or unwanted. However, permissive parenting such as over-controlling or insensitive behavior can also play an important role in influencing Narcissism disorder.

Although to find out the exact cause of this personality disorder is complex to figure out but, the children who have been raised by a Narcissist are more likely to develop Narcissism disorder. Although parental narcissism can affect the children but even with few maternal narcissistic traits has the ability to affect their daughters in deceptive ways.

Well, if you are new to the realization of a maternal narcissism then you need to keep learning about what you have to deal with. One of the worst things which you may come to know is the fact that your narcissist parent will never change until she finds a way to bring healthier change in her life.

Well to know what signs and symptoms of maternal narcissism can be and how it can affect you, it is highly important to learn about this in a proper way. Well, here we have brought major and most common symptoms of maternal narcissism which are surely going to be better for you to know in this regard.

# Conclusion

Energy vampires – they'll make you feel like you owe them the world, including your own sense of security, self-esteem, and confidence. They'll make every day an obstacle course, an elaborate maze to navigate with extreme caution. Make the wrong turn, and you could be face to face with their demons.

Much like the typical image of pop culture vampires throughout the years, real-life energy vampires can be seductive, admirable, pleasant, and charismatic. They ooze an appeal that begs to be praised, and we just can't help but give them the attention that they so obviously deserve... at a glance.

It's because of their superb capability to present themselves in the best way possible that makes it easy for the rest of us to feel captivated and fall in love. We gravitate towards them, we offer ourselves up to them, we try to be a part of their life because we want that perfection to rub off on us. But when the smoke clears away, and the mask is pulled off, the real narcissist shows its true form.

Behind closed doors, these individuals can be the worst to deal with. They'll make you feel like everything is your fault and they'll make you doubt your own capabilities and talents.

They'll destroy your reputation and your relationships without thinking twice, and they'll laugh at you when it's all over. They'll control you and take your identity, they'll force you to toe a tight line and whip you back in shape when you make the tiniest misstep.

They're not easy to deal with, and they're definitely not yours to fix.

At the end of the day, the narcissist in your life will not change. Accept that. Don't think that it was ever your responsibility to make them a better person. It never was. What you need to think about is your own self-worth, your emotional wellness, and your mental well-being.

You are your own responsibility, and you need to protect yourself from the vampires around you.

So, take this information as your wooden stake and drive it through the heart of the relationship you've been trying to save. Before anyone else, save yourself from the abuse and give yourself the chance at a better life and better relationships – there are far more people out there who would gladly give you what you truly deserve without any strings attached.

Is it easy to live life without the abuser you've come to know and love? Absolutely not. But remember, you can't pour from an empty vessel. Restore yourself first and do away with the people who sap you of what you have to give. This should help you find your way to more fruitful, more loving relationships that will reciprocate the affection and positivity you have to share.

www.ingramcontent.com/pod-product-compliance
Lightning Source LLC
Chambersburg PA
CBHW070800040426
42333CB00060B/1412